Rug Hooking
MADE EASY

Rug Hooking
MADE EASY

By Charlotte Kimball Stratton

Illustrated

HARPER & ROW, PUBLISHERS

New York and Evanston

RUG HOOKING MADE EASY

Lithographed by The Murray Printing Co., Forge Village, Mass.

Library of Congress catalog card number: 55–10704

To

my lifelong rug-hooking friends in Vermont,
to my newer friends from all parts of our country,
and to my family, whose encouragement and assistance
have made this book possible

Table of Contents

Table of Contents

List of Color Plates

The following color photographs will be found after page 64:

Foreword

The renaissance of handicraft has been accelerated in recent years by the increasing amount of free time available for personal interests and hobbies. For many, this means doing something creative; making something worth while; the satisfaction of an urge to create articles of value and beauty for the adornment of the home; or the sheer pleasure of working with the hands. The escape from routine is another factor giving impetus to the arts and crafts movement.

It is gratifying to find many groups who have banded together for mutual creative interests. Adult classes conducted by public school, community and church groups, private classes and summer workshops can be found in various communities. Many values are apparent to me in relation to these classes. Perhaps the social value is the most important as derived through congenial contact, comradery in classes and the interchange of ideas. Excellent and lasting friendships have evolved from such groups. The shorter work week and earlier retirement have been great factors in the development and continuation of these classes. It has become increasingly apparent that people need to be educated to retire to worth-while activity and not merely retire from activity.

Rug hooking is one of the most popular crafts to interest groups or individuals. It is encouraging to note that a recognized authority and leading craftsman teacher in this field is willing to share her knowledge and experience with others. We gain satisfaction and a sense of accomplishment only by sharing with others. I know it is with this spirit of leading others into stimulating and worth-while activity that the author has been motivated to express her craft through publication.

KENNETH H. LUNDY, Consultant,
Arts and Crafts Education,
Connecticut State Department of Education

Tribute

A person who gives a lifetime to the study, development and advancement of a craft, as Charlotte K. Stratton has given to hooked rugs and their making, contributes lasting benefits to such a craft.

Mrs. Stratton, in her enthusiasm and zeal, has ferreted out the true history of hooked rugs. She has found the best methods of making them through the years, all the while teaching thousands of women throughout the United States to make heirloom rugs for their homes.

The making of hooked rugs has been greatly advanced through the search and intelligent application of this one woman's methods. Her book, a labor of love, will delight everyone privileged to enjoy its pages.

MARY BROOKS PICKEN

3 Nelson Street
Montpelier, Vermont
November 15, 1954

Dear Dot:

As one of the many who attended your classes I would like to speak for all of them to express our deep and sincere gratitude to you for the wonderful hours we spent at your Vermont studio.

It was my privilege to act as the first chairman of a Montpelier group, a position which I had the honor to hold as long as the studio was in operation. It was an experience that was most pleasant and of great value to me in the work of carrying on the rug work in Montpelier and Burlington after you closed your studio.

Your influence for perfect rug work was so firmly established in our minds we can never forget it. Your conduct of the studio with never an unpleasant moment is one of our fondest memories. When classes meet, as they have continued to do since you moved to Massachusetts, someone always speaks of "Dot" and our fondness for you.

We all know that you have gone far in the field of hooked rugs since leaving Vermont, that you are now a national figure and we all wish you the greatest success in any venture that you may undertake.

(Signed)   Mrs. Abbie L. Starkey

Acknowledgments

The author wishes to express her appreciation to her pupils, to the graduates of her teachers' normal school and to her many friends who have so generously loaned their rugs for the illustrations shown. To list the names of all of these persons is not possible in this section of the book but full credit is given to the hooker with each illustration.

Special appreciation is given to Mr. Kenneth H. Lundy of the Connecticut State Department of Education for his token of friendship for me as expressed in the foreword.

The tribute from Mary Brooks Picken, noted author of the *Singer Sewing Book* and some ninety other equally fine publications, touches a very warm spot in my heart and indicates the true friendship of a wonderful lady.

The tribute from my Vermont friends as sent me by Mrs. Abbie L. Starkey of Montpelier, Vermont, is most gratifying and sincerely appreciated.

For the opportunity to use on the jacket of this book one of my favorite designs, my sincere thanks to Mrs. Delta Harmon of Longmeadow, Massachusetts, whose teacher was Mrs. Ruth Henrich, East Longmeadow, Massachusetts, a graduate of the Charlotte K. Stratton Teachers Normal School.

Special thanks are due to other owners who graciously loaned their rugs to be specially photographed for the color plates included in this book. Plate IV shows "Roumanian Convent," hooked by Mrs. Marie Hutchins, Springfield, Massachusetts, at the Yankee Peddler Studio in Montpelier, Vermont. Each of the other rugs shown in the color plates were hooked by a graduate of the Charlotte K. Stratton Teachers Normal School, as follows:

"Vermont Fireplace Rug" by Mrs. Ella Goodrich, Greenfield, Massachusetts

"Antoinette's Bridal Rug" by Mrs. Mildred Millhouse, West Hartford, Connecticut

"Persian Oriental" by Miss Frieda Powers, Bernardston, Massachusetts

"Turkish Oriental" by Mrs. Blanche Godfrey, Gardner, Massachusetts

"Priscilla Pansies" by Mrs. Alice Croteau, Northampton, Massachusetts

"Summer Bloom" by Mrs. Florence Peck, Newtown, Connecticut

The Color Circle is used by courtesy of the Munsell Color Co. of Baltimore, Maryland, and in my chapter on color are excerpts from Munsell publications.

I am indebted to the expert skill and patient efforts of Herb Shumway of Greenfield, Massachusetts, for the black and white photographs reproduced in this book. Though he poses as an amateur photographer his work is that of a real professional.

And to the many other friends who have assisted with suggestions and encouragement, my very sincere thanks. If by chance anyone has been omitted I assure you it was not intentional.

Introduction

During the past few years a number of books on rug hooking have been published by various authorities on the subject. They are all good but it is of course only natural that each author reflects something of his or her own personality and tastes in their writing.

I can be excused therefore if, in this book, I put before you my personal ideas gleaned from early training in art and design and many years of experience in adapting that early knowledge to the art of making hooked rugs.

I use the word "art" advisedly because my training with water colors, oils and crayons has been of such great value to me in producing the subtle shading of scrolls, leaves or flowers. And it is of invaluable assistance in transferring my knowledge to hookers who are preparing themselves to be teachers or just hooking hobbyists.

My personal choice of strip width is $\frac{3}{32}$ inch and most of the rugs illustrated were hooked with that type of wool strip. However, I would not disapprove of any width of cloth, whether hooked high or low. Each hooker has his or her preference, just as we all have our likes and dislikes in food, clothing, etc. After all, the most important point in making a hooked rug is the pleasure and satisfaction each one of us derives in producing an article of beauty and value with our own hands in the manner we ourselves like.

In my opinion, there is much pleasure and personal satisfaction in knowing something of the background of hooked rugs. Therefore I have included a chapter on Frost, the Yankee Peddler.

In the course of your hooked rug work you will find rug patterns depicting the art of the American Indian and the Pennsylvania Dutch along with all other types of art. Some of them are really unique. The designs of the Navaho Indians are usually geometric in their formation, as they follow the woven blanket designs, an art in which the Navahos are experts. The Pennsylvania Dutch designs are of a very different character. Though crude in construction they served as a means of expressing their love of decorative ornamentation and appeared on their buildings, furniture, pottery and other objects of the craftsman's skill.

A study of the Navaho and Pennsylvania Dutch arts, from books obtainable at your public library, is both interesting and instructive. As I have indicated the use of Paisley in much of the instruction, a knowledge of the origin of the Paisley shawl and the life of the weavers in Paisley, Scotland, would also be helpful in your work. To broaden your knowledge of design, I recommend these studies.

The purpose of this book is, as the title indicates, to make your rug hooking easy and pleasurable, to acquire knowledge of the fundamentals of hooking and skill in execution, or perhaps to perfect the knowledge you already have.

When ready to use the pages on instruction, study the particular motif you are to hook and keep the book on or near your frame for ready reference. The steps in hooking each type of motif, flower, leaf, scroll or whatever, are given as clearly as possible. Follow the directions carefully and I am sure you will be pleased with the results. The increased interest in your work and the quality of your hooking will be helpful to your teacher.

Rug Hooking
MADE EASY

❦ 1 ❧

Design

What is the meaning of the word design? It is not a new term; in fact it is centuries old, although in prehistoric times probably the creator of objects or the decoration thereon did not describe them with the word design.

The word may be used in two very distinct ways; constructive and decorative. Constructive or structural designs possess solid form or shape. Decorative designs refer to the combination of lines, either straight or curved, which are used to embellish and beautify a structural object which may or may not in itself be an object of beauty.

Since the subject of this book is the making of hooked rugs, we are particularly interested in decorative design rather than structural. This being the case, we can forget the form or shape of our hooked rug and devote our whole attention to the means by which we change a drab piece of burlap to an article of beauty as well as usefulness.

Design, then, as we use the term, is a combination of straight and curved lines into something that will be pleasing to the eye and satisfy our creative instincts. When this combination of lines, which has produced a design, is joined with many other combinations the whole is also spoken of as a design.

The ancient cave dwellers recorded the history of their daily life in the crude designs carved on the walls of their abodes. It was their way of speaking to those generations who followed them in a language which would be understood.

I like to think of design as a language which speaks to us in a manner that we hookers all understand just as much as though it were the spoken or written word. In art training we are first taught to use only pencil lines, studying to feel and live the story they are telling us.

There are six elements to design which are generally termed as line, direction, shape, proportion or measure, texture, and color. These elements start our thinking of design as the A B C's give us the key to our first attempts at reading. I call these six elements "the scales of graphic expression."

To many observers the straight line is positive; to me it expresses direction. A curved line seems active and graceful. A zigzag line gives the effect of an emotional disturbance.

Direction. It seems all lines have a destination or direction, whether horizontal, vertical or oblique. I was taught that a horizontal line has a quiet and calm effect while a vertical line helped to produce balance.

Shape is the contour produced by the boundary lines of a figure or motif, such as the square, triangle, diamond, circle, etc.

Measure is illustrated by contrast between a long and short line or a large and small figure while proportion is the ratio of one line or figure to another. Incorrect ratio would be an overlarge design next to a tiny one.

Texture is as important in design as color. Texture in paintings, fabrics, metals, plastics, clothing, etc., plays an important part in our daily selections for designed living.

Now, having given consideration to some of the basic principles of design, let's apply them to our hooked rug. If you are planning to draw your own design, the principles given above should be of assistance to you. If, however, you prefer to select a pattern from the many commercial designs on the market, these same principles should have a bearing on your choice.

In reviewing the basic principles consider the line, its direction, the shape of the figure which the line produces and the proportion or ratio of one figure or motif to others in the design. If the design has a scroll-type border whose main theme is an S-type curve, be sure that the theme is carried out in a graceful manner. As a concrete example, let us take my pattern No. 451, Nichols Fernery, a quarter of which is shown in Fig. 1.

Fig. 1.   Design No. 451, "Nichols Fernery"

Note the graceful curve on the main vein in each fern scroll and the pleasing contour of each separate frond. Note also that I introduced the fern in the center design, which I find produces a favorable balance of the whole. And, in keeping with the theme of gracefulness, the center design is bordered by an arched ribbon. Here is an opportunity for you to train your eye to notice the important features of good design. For example: the arcs of the ribbon are in conformity with the S curve of the fern veins. All of this helps you to understand the rhythm of lines in design.

The rose which is in all four corners is also included in the center bouquet. And the leaves surrounding the rose are not stiff and flat but are curved, which gives them the life that appears in nature, again carrying out the curve of other parts of the design.

In a previous paragraph I mentioned that some hookers enjoy making their own patterns and do so. Others would like to but do not have the courage to try their luck as they are perhaps lacking in art training or a natural talent in this field. To this group I would recommend starting with some simple geometric designs which almost anyone with a little patience could draw. You will be surprised at the real beauty of such designs when proper colors are used in hooking them.

Let me repeat, "Design is a pleasing combination of straight and curved lines."

For illustration let us take the straight-line designs first:

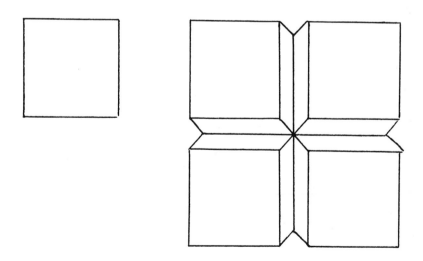

FIG. 2. The square, when amplified with a few more straight lines, produces a block or box design

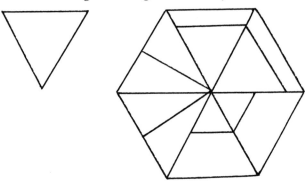

Fig. 3. The triangle. When we add more triangles, we have a hexagonal or six-sided design. Variations are almost unlimited

❧ 2 ❧

Color

Earliest man obtained his color pigments from minerals and the juices of insects and plants. His colors were few and in striking contrast and were used to decorate his body, his crude pottery articles and his abode. The war paint of the American Indian and the elaborate body decoration of the medicine man, as an assistance in driving out evil spirits, are typical examples of the early American use of color. The ancient Egyptians and Phoenicians were among the earliest people to make extensive use of color. Chapter 1 of *The Science of Color,* by the Colorimetry Committee of the Optical Society of America (John Wiley and Sons, New York) is an excellent reference.

It was not until 1928 that the first synthetic colors were developed. From this first step countless new artificial colors have been given the modern world through chemistry. And some authorities claim that we have only scratched the surface in this field as still more and more colors are being developed.

Ever since the world began there have undoubtedly been sunshine and rain, and when the two occur at the same time there has always been a rainbow caused by the white rays of sunlight being broken up as they passed through the drops of rain. This is a phenomenon of nature with which we are all familiar.

However, it was not until 1666 that Sir Isaac Newton discovered that with a man-made article, the glass prism, he could produce an artificial rainbow showing the same spectrum colors but with slightly different wave lengths.

The complete science of color is so vast and far-reaching it could not possibly be included in a treatise of the nature and purpose of this book, and to the average rug hooker it is not of interest. To those who enjoy digging to the bottom of a subject I recommend some of the many very fine books by writers who have spent years in this most interesting study. Recommended reading: *Science of Color* by the Colorimetry Committee of the Optical Society of America (John Wiley & Sons, New York); *Principles of Color and Color Mixing* by J. H. Bustanoby (McGraw-Hill Book Co.,

Inc., New York); *An Introduction to Colour* by T. Elder Dickson (Pitman), now out of print but available in large libraries.

Color harmony. This is a subject of vital interest to the rug hooker and of great importance in selecting the colors for the different motifs in the design of her pattern as well as the background.

We have learned from experience that certain color combinations are pleasing to the eye and mind while others give offense. The first group are known as "harmonies" while the latter are known as "discords."

Color harmony, however, is not only a matter of selection but also of arrangement. This fact is not as commonly recognized as it should be among rug hookers. Too often the color selection may be very good but the arrangement of the colors in the rug may disturb the whole balance. It is well to remember that "colors change in effect" by the colors adjacent to them.

Unfortunately there are no definite rules or laws governing perfect harmony in color combinations as suitability and personal taste enter in. Color scales or wheels serve to train the eye to pleasing arrangement.

I am indebted to the Munsell Color Co. of Baltimore, Maryland, for their assistance and permission to include in this book excerpts from some of their publications. The Munsell System of Color Notation is used by science and industry for evaluating various products and certain phenomena in terms of color. Specifications for hay, cotton, tomatoes and many other agricultural products include Munsell notations as the standard reference for grading colors.

The arts (and rug hooking is an art) also benefit by the Munsell System of Color Notation. An artist who is sufficiently familiar with the system may record the color notation of a particular scene on a rough sketch and reproduce those colors accurately at his leisure.

QUALITIES OF COLOR SENSATION

The following explanation of the three distinct qualities of color sensation, hue, value and chroma, is quoted from *Color Notation* by A. H. Munsell (Munsell Color Co., Inc., 10 E. Franklin St., Baltimore, Md.). I highly recommend this book to rug hookers as a condensed, easily understood treatise on the subject of color.

A child gathers flowers, hoards colored beads, chases butterflies and begs for the gaudiest painted toys. At first his strong color sensations are sufficiently described by the simple terms red, yellow, blue, green and purple. But he soon sees that some are light, while others are dark, and later he comes to perceive that each hue has many degrees. Thus he early recognizes three ways in which color differs. Consciously or not, all skillful use of color must reckon with these simple but important facts.

Every color sensation unites three distinct attributes, defined as hue, value and chroma. One quality may be varied without disturbing the others. Thus, a color may be weakened or strengthened in chroma without changing its value or hue. Or its hue may be modified without changing its value or chroma and, finally, its value may be changed without effecting its hue or chroma.

Hue is that attribute by which we distinguish one "color family" from another, as red from yellow or green from blue or purple. It is the difference in length of ether waves striking on the retina of the eye which causes the sensation of color.

Value is the quality of lightness or darkness of a color. We loosely speak of color values as tints and shades but these terms are frequently misapplied. A tint should be a light value and a shade a dark value, but the word shade has become a general term for any type of color so that a shade of yellow may prove to be lighter than a tint of blue.

Chroma is that quality of color by which we distinguish a strong color from a weak one; the degree of departure of a color sensation from that of white or grey; the intensity of a distinctive hue. Much of the popular misunderstanding of color is caused by ignorance of those three dimensions or by an attempt to make two dimensions do the work of three.

I suggest to every rug hooker that you make an effort to familiarize yourself with these simple but important qualities of color. Such knowledge will be of much assistance in selecting the colors and their arrangement in your hooked rug.

CLASSIFICATIONS OF COLOR

Most readers of this book (and certainly the rug hookers) will be familiar with the accepted classification of colors as primary, secondary, adjacent and complementary. Still, a brief review will not be amiss.

The term *primary* is given to red, yellow and blue because they cannot be made from any mixtures of pigments.

Secondary colors are those produced by the mixture of two primary colors. Red plus yellow gives orange; red plus blue gives violet and blue plus yellow gives green. The secondary colors are therefore, orange, violet and green.

Adjacent colors are those near to each other in the hue circle and in a degree similar to each other; for example, yellow and green. Both contain yellow and are therefore related. If two related hues are mixed together the result will be a hue similar to both; for example, blue and green will produce blue-green.

Complementary colors. From my experience in training teachers of hooked rug work I have found that the term "complementary" is often misunderstood. *Funk and Wagnalls Standard Dictionary* defines the adjective "complementary" as "serving as a complement" and the noun "complement" is defined as "something that fills up or completes." Too often the word "complementary" is confused with "compl*i*mentary" which has an entirely different meaning; "flattering" or "admiring."

Complementary colors are directly across from each other in the hue circle. They are opposite in their very nature and there is no similarity in the colorants from which they are made. For example, the complementary of blue is orange, which is made from yellow and red. When complementary colors are placed near to each other the strength or intensity of each *appears* to increase. Combinations of colors at full intensity are too brilliant or garish and should be subdued or softened by mixing in grey or an opposing color.

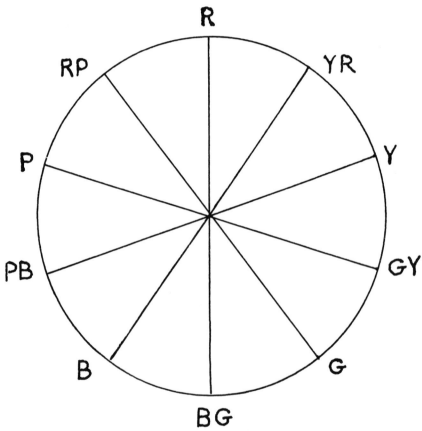

FIG. 4.   Color Circle (Courtesy of Munsell Color Company)

❧ 3 ❧

Dyes and Dyeing

To many present-day hookers one of the great joys of making a hooked rug is the planning of the colors and then spending a day with the dye pot using the multitude of dye colors already prepared for her.

Grandmother did not bother with graduated shades of any one color but produced various reds from different herbs and fruits even though they were not of the same family of reds. Today's hooker wishes more subtle effects in her flowers and scrolls and, with modern dye formulas properly used in proper containers, she is able to produce many shades and tints of each color she wishes to use.

As our first consideration is the powdered dye, which we purchase in attractive envelopes, a word about them seems appropriate. The two leading dye manufacturers in this country are Du Pont and General Dyestuffs. There may be some differences in the methods by which the two companies produce their dyes but in general they are the same. Each dye company has its own names for the dyes it manufactures. It either combines certain dyes for the retailers or sells them separately to be mixed by the retailers.

Two retailers of prominence in this field are the W. Cushing Company of Dover-Foxcroft, Maine, and Putnam Dye Company of Quincy, Illinois. I am familiar with and have used both Cushing and Putnam dyes. They are equally good. New Englanders are accustomed to the Cushing dye packages because they are locally made and easily obtained. Some hookers who have tried the Putnam dyes have not always been pleased with the results. Perhaps the reason is that, while each company may sell a package marked "American Beauty," the mixture of reds in each one may be quite different. American Beauty is not a raw dye; it is merely a name given to a mixture of raw dyes to produce a color that would primarily be used to hook an American Beauty rose as well as other motifs of a design.

MY METHOD OF DYEING

With the four pans illustrated I dye four shades at one time, each shade in its own dye pot. I never use a solution the second time because the cloth should have absorbed practically all of the dye in the solution, and chemists tell me that "second-hand" dyes will not produce so clear a shade. Therefore, mix only the quantity necessary for the particular job.

In order to give you the best possible formulas for your dyeing I solicited the help of Mr. Jack Allen of Barrington, Rhode Island, a well-known technician in this field. I am indebted to him for the formulas given below. I told Mr. Allen which colors I wished, and he worked out the proper formula. It was unusual for him to do this but I have a deep friendship for Mr. and Mrs. Allen and wherever I go with my Yankee Peddler Pageant of beautiful hooked rugs the Allen swatches go with me to help those hookers who do not care to do the dyeing themselves. Often a hooker will have bad luck with her dyeing and buy a swatch to fill in.

Fig. 5. Dyeing equipment

GENERAL INSTRUCTIONS

Material: 6 x 18 inch strips of bleached White wool flannel, weighing 14 oz. per yard.

Stock solution: One package of Perfection Dye dissolved in 1½ qts. of water, cooled to get good solution.

Dye bath: In each pan put sufficient water to completely cover the material to be dyed. Add *one teaspoon table salt* and *one tablespoon white vinegar.*

To this solution add the required amount of stock solution. Soak flannel thoroughly in warm water and wring it before adding to the dye bath. Bring slowly to a boil, stirring the goods continually. Boiling is continued for 30 minutes, after which the goods are washed in cold water, then dried away from direct heat.

Copy above directions regardless of color used.

As an example of dyeing six shades we will take Olive Green.

Shade 1 (the lightest shade)—use ⅛ teaspoon of stock solution.
Shade 2—⅔ teaspoon stock solution.
Shade 3—2 teaspoons stock solution.
Shade 4—2 tablespoons stock solution.
Shade 5—4 tablespoons stock solution.
Shade 6—8 tablespoons stock solution.

If desired, instead of using Shade 1, which is very light, begin with Shade 2. Proceed as above for Shades 2–6. Make an additional shade by using 16 tablespoons of the stock solution.

The following colors were also tested for me: Old Gold, Green, Blue, Pink, Red Grape. The above formulas for six shades of Olive Green apply to any of these colors. There are just six shades. We sometimes call them in numerical order from 1, the lightest, to 6, the darkest. We may also number them from each end toward the middle: that is, lightest, 2nd light, 3rd light; then darkest, 2nd dark and 3rd dark.

A PLEASING BACKGROUND FORMULA

Fig. 58 shows one of my designs, "Maine Cone & Tassel," hooked by Mrs. Genevieve Pont Briand of Northampton, Massachusetts. The design was also hooked by Mrs. Sadie E. Starkey of Templeton, Massachusetts, and it is to her that I am indebted for the background formula here given.

Mrs. Starkey writes me that she used ½ lb. of medium shade Tan coating material cut in strips about 6 inches x 12 inches. In four quarts of water she dissolved 1½ teaspoons Maroon, ¾ teaspoon Mulberry, ½ teaspoon Navy, 3¼ teaspoons Black. She set the color with vinegar, 2 tablespoons per quart of water. She then made a new bath of water and vinegar and placed the dyed pieces in it and boiled them. These are directions for dyeing ½ lb. of material. Repeat the dyeing until you have the quantity required for a particular design. I allow ½ lb. of wool to each square foot of burlap. I do not subtract the area of the design. It is better to have some left over than to run short. If a hooker is wasteful, I advise an extra pound.

MULTIPLE-SHADE DYEING

Through the courtesy of Mrs. Sherman Ives, a well-known hooked rug instructor of Thomaston, Connecticut, I am privileged to give you directions for multiple-shade dyeing. Mrs. Ives has evolved this method to fit

the needs of her pupils in hooking small flowers, leaves, etc., which are required only in limited quantities.

Basic formula: ½ teaspoon *dry* powdered dye, ½ cup boiling water.

Materials needed: Jars of basic formulas of colors desired; shallow enameled basin; one strip of White wool, thoroughly soaked and wrung dry; salt (pure); measuring spoons.

Now for the actual dyeing. Use one piece of White, approximately 4 x 12 inches, for each shade, and dye the strips separately.

Going from light to medium dark

<blockquote>
Shade 1—1 cup water plus ⅛ tsp. basic formula.
Shade 2—1 cup water plus ¼ tsp. basic formula.
Shade 3—1 cup water plus ¾ tsp. basic formula.
Shade 4—1 cup water plus 1½ tsp. basic formula.
Shade 5—1 cup water plus 2¾ tsp. basic formula.
Shade 6—1 cup water plus 4 tsp. basic formula.
Shade 7—1 cup water plus 6 tsp. basic formula.
Shade 8—1 cup water plus 8 tsp. basic formula.
Shade 9—1 cup water plus 10 tsp. basic formula.
Shade 10—1 cup water plus 13 tsp. basic formula.
</blockquote>

This shading is so gradual you have to skip to every other one or to every third one in order really to see the gradation, but using all shades makes for fine work.

Shade 11—Use 8th shade plus a pinch of dry Black or Green or Brown or Blue (depending on the hue you are dyeing) to deepen it.

<blockquote>
Shade 12—9 plus a pinch as in 11th shade.
Shade 13—10 plus a pinch as in 11th shade.
Shade 14—13 plus a pinch of dry dye in shade of deeper color.
</blockquote>

For example: if you are using Sky Blue, for the 11th shade add a pinch of Navy Blue, also for 12th and 13th shade. But for the 14th shade use 13 plus Black and you will get a still deeper shade of Blue, making 14 beautifully graduated shades in blue.

FIG. 6. Design No. 251, "Concord." Hooked by Harold Ransom, Hartford, Connecticut

Fig. 7. Frost Design No. 4. Hooked by the author

FIG. 8. Frost Design No. 59. Hooked by Mrs. Dorothy Lincoln, Montpelier, Vermont

FIG. 9. Frost Design No. 11. Hooked by the author

SPOT DYEING

Many hookers enjoy using "spot-dyed" materials. The following directions are also given through the courtesy of Mrs. Sherman Ives.

Add to your materials a medicine dropper.

1. Put one cup of water in dyeing basin, add color you wish for basic color (such as, 1 teaspoon basic formula in Gold). Bring to rolling boil.

2. Immerse White strip (approximately 4 inches x 12 inches) which has been thoroughly soaked in warm water and wrung out dry, leaving as much surface exposed as possible.

3. Salt (about 1 teaspoon) as soon as desired shade is obtained.

4. Then take ½ teaspoon basic formula of Cardinal and dribble from the teaspoon or medicine dropper over as much of exposed surface as possible to give a splotchy appearance.

5. *Add immediately* about 1½ teaspoons pure salt.

Follow steps 4 and 5 until all colors you wish to spot are used up.

(The secret in beautiful spot dyeing is *little water* in the basin, and *immediate* salting to hold the colors where you want them.)

6. Turn burner low, partially cover with lid and simmer for 20 minutes.

(One has to watch this pretty closely or it will scorch, especially if it is a day when water boils away quickly.)

7. Rinse thoroughly so all excess dye and salt are removed, first in warm water, gradually reducing to cold. Dry and press.

I find in almost all cases that this quantity of dye and size of cloth successfully use up the dye. The water is almost always clear when completed, as the right amounts of dye have been used for the cloth to take up the color.

DYE FORMULA FOR CARDINAL POPPY WITH WHITE EDGE

This formula is by courtesy of Mrs. Mabel Miller of Plantsville, Connecticut, a graduate of my Normal School for Hooked Rug Teachers. Mrs. Miller conducts classes in her section of Connecticut and has been most successful. Fig. 10 is my design "Antique Poppies," pattern No. 209, which Mrs. Miller hooked with exceptional ability.

1. Dissolve one package Perfection Cardinal Dye in 1 quart boiling water.

2. Into each of four 1½- or 2-quart pans pour 1 quart cold water and place each pan on a burner of the range.

3. To pan 1 add ⅛ teaspoon of basic Cardinal solution; in pan 2, ¼ teaspoon; in pan 3, ½ teaspoon; in pan 4, 1½ teaspoons. Also, into each pan, one teaspoon pure salt.

4. Tear medium-weight White wool into 12-inch squares and saturate in warm water.

5. When dye bath begins to boil, add a square of the White wool to each pan, stir well and continue stirring and simmering for 20 minutes. Rinse each square in clear water and dry.

This completes the first four shades.

6. Proceed in this manner for Shades 5, 6, 7, 8, 9, and 10, using the following quantities of basic solution.

> Shade 5—four teaspoons.
> Shade 6—three tablespoons.
> Shade 7—½ cup.
> Shade 8—½ cup and one tablespoon Dark Grey.
> Shade 9—½ cup and five tablespoons Dark Grey.
> Shade 10—½ cup and ½ cup Dark Grey.

For the Grey edges of petals:

Substitute in Cardinal instructions 1, 2, 3 same quantity of Silver Grey, taking particular care that Shade 3 of the Grey has the same color value as Shade 3 of the Cardinal. It might possibly be necessary to use the 4th shade of Grey to have a good blend from the Cardinal into the Grey.

Fig. 10. Design No. 209, "Antique Poppies." Hooked by Mrs. Mabel Miller, Plantsville, Connecticut

❧ 4 ❧

Equipment and Care of Hooked Rugs

FRAME

If you wish to use a floor-model frame there are several different types on the market. These may be obtained either through your teacher or your department store, or you may send direct to the manufacturer. Each type has it special features and they are all good. Just be sure they are sturdy and well constructed in all parts. Various sizes are available but the average standard size is 40 inches. This size will accommodate the average scatter rug pattern and room-size rugs may also be hooked in two or three strips using this frame instead of one large 6 x 9 foot or 9 x 12 foot piece of burlap.

If circumstances make it necessary to have your frame "home-made" be sure that whoever does the work makes your frame the proper height and has the easel part the correct width. Accuracy in these details may save shoulder or back strain when the frame is used. Soft wood is best, as hardwood is cumbersome to take to class.

To avoid slippage of the rollers, ratchet-type metals may be procured

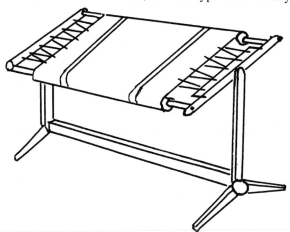

FIG. 11. Floor-model hooking frame

41

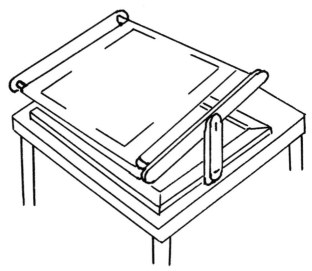

FIG. 12.   Stratton table-model folding rug frame

from frame manufacturers. These ratchets are notched metal pieces inserted at each end of the rollers to mesh with similar ratchets placed on the side pieces of the easel part of the frame. Fig. 11 is an example of a good sturdy floor model.

Nearly all hookers enjoy making small articles, such as chair seats, pictures, hand bags, etc. For such work many prefer a small table-model folding frame like the one shown in Fig. 12.

This frame is a new product my company (the Charlotte K. Stratton Company) manufactures and its reception by hookers from many parts of the country has been most gratifying. When not in use it folds easily and compactly and can be stored in a much smaller space than the floor model. It is light in weight and easily transported. The 30-inch model will accommodate a pattern up to 30 inches in width, or a larger pattern if in two strips as many of my new designs are now being made. The trend with hookers seems to be toward the small-type frame because of the special features mentioned above, and it pleases me to know that I was the first to present its type to the hookers.

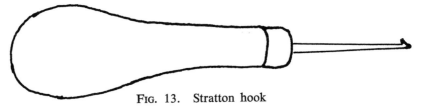

FIG. 13.   Stratton hook

HOOK

Your hook can be obtained from a department store and there are several models available. Several years ago I designed the handle of the hook made by my company; it is shaped to fit the average hooker's hand. Before being put on the market it was tested by many hookers and, even after eight hours of continuous hooking, there were no ill effects on the hand muscles. But, if your hook handle is too large or too small, the muscles of the hand are strained in trying to hold it.

LACING SET

There must be some method of mounting your burlap pattern on the rug frame. Many hookers use silk hose or similar material to fasten the burlap to the sides of the frame. This method will suffice if the hose are attached to the burlap at very frequent intervals. If not so fastened, there will be a tendency toward a wavy instead of a perfectly straight edge on the finished rug.

I personally enjoy using my lacing set illustrated in Fig. 12. The burlap is at all times held straight and taut in the frame, making your hooking much easier and giving loops of evener height. It is very popular with thousands of hookers and, because of the excellent canvas of which it is made, it will last almost forever. I always urge a new hooker to have her original equipment as good as can be obtained even though her first pattern is only a chair seat. The equipment can be used over and over.

PATTERN

In choosing your first pattern there are a few important points to consider. As the life of your rug, or other hooked article, is the life of the base on which it is hooked, be sure that the burlap is of excellent quality. In selection of a design bear in mind the place in which the finished rug or other article is to be used. Be sure that the drawing is clear and distinct and the printing is of a permanent nature.

I always advise a beginner to start her hobby with a small design, one that she can finish in a comparatively short time. The hooker is quite likely to become discouraged if she attempts to hook even a medium-sized rug as her first venture. A finished chair-seat design, if well done, will bring compliments and praise from family friends and she will be encouraged to continue. The completion of one's first project is a great reward. It also prevents others from saying, "She's had that big rug going for a year and it isn't done yet."

STRIP SLITTER

Until a few years ago the hooker cut all of her wool materials with hand shears. This method was slow and laborious. Now some smart fellow has invented a machine to do this work, saving time as well as a lot of physical effort. You may still use the hand method if you desire, but a machine will give you much more even cuttings. There are several now on the market, in quite a wide price range. They all operate easily and will last a long time. If the cutter head becomes dull it may be exchanged for a new one at a nominal cost. Sometimes a group of neighbor hookers chip together to buy the higher-priced models, but if you are doing a lot of hooking yourself it is much more satisfactory to have your own machine. The best hand shears for this work are the Wiss Bent Rug Shears which retail for about $3.25.

For some time after the First World War these shears were not obtainable, but at this writing they are back on the market. If you own a pair, do not use them for any purpose except cutting materials for your rug.

CARE OF HOOKED RUGS

The care of your hooked rug begins right at the start of hooking it. Correct mounting, taut and *even,* eliminates pressing or steaming when finished.

The burlap, if of excellent quality, has a sizing which is used in the surface finishing process. This should be preserved as carefully as possible. Moisture of any kind will destroy this sizing; therefore do not steam or wash your hooked rug. If it becomes soiled from use, shampoo it with a good brand of rug or upholstery cleanser following directions on the container and using the *foam* only, not the liquid part of the solution.

And if your rug is a rather choice piece, and a great many of them are, don't use it where the traffic is too heavy. Use them, of course, but with discretion.

✿ 5 ✿

Preparation of Pattern

BINDING A ROUND DESIGN

We will assume you have selected Geometric Chair Seat Design No. 54 (Fig. 8). The design will be in a circle, as illustrated, stamped on a square piece of burlap. Any round or oval pattern will require a binding on the edge. This is done as follows:

Place the right side of the binding on the outside border of the right side of the burlap and baste together. Be sure to ease the binding as you baste it, so as not to draw on the pattern when finally turned back. Please note, this method of binding before hooking is done exactly as you would bind a circular skirt.

Stitch the binding evenly on the line of the round or oval pattern. Turn binding back flat on the surplus burlap and lightly baste so that the binding will not interfere with your hooking right up to the binding. This will give an excellent finish to the edge of the chair seat or rug.

When hooking is completed, remove basting threads and cut off the surplus burlap just inside the edge of the binding, not too close to the stitching. Hem closely to the back of the finished article. *Do not cut away* the surplus burlap until you have finished hooking.

You are now ready to attach your burlap to the lacing set. The Stratton lacing set, made of heavy canvas, can be used to attach the burlap securely to any rug frame. It consists of two 17-inch side eyelet pieces and two 38½-inch pieces to attach the burlap to frame rollers. Two lacing cords are also included. Hold together the right sides of the burlap and one of the long pieces of the lacing set, centers matched, and overcast with heavy button thread, working from the center toward each end. Repeat with the other long piece and the other end of the burlap. Stitches should be placed close together.

Tack each of the long green canvas strips to the rollers of your frame using #8 carpet tacks, spacing tacks about an inch apart. Tack short eyelet pieces of lacing set to sides of frame being sure eyelets are inside.

If the burlap is longer than the distance between the rollers, roll enough of the pattern onto the upper roller so that the lower edge of the design is within the frame where you can easily hook it. Be sure the burlap is good and taut. Lace side pieces to the burlap with the cord included with the set.

HEMMING A SQUARE-CORNERED PATTERN BEFORE ATTACHING TO FRAME

To prepare a square-cornered pattern before attaching it to the frame, I use the following method. First, cut off any surplus burlap outside border-line of the pattern. Taking the short side of the burlap, fold back to the outside line of the design and firmly press. Be sure to fold straight and even *just on the line* as shown in 1, Fig. 14. Do not make a fold on the ragged edge. Next, fold the corners as shown in 2 and cut off the corner end of the fold leaving about one-half inch. Now, fold long sides of burlap on the outside borderline of the design and press straight and firm. Your burlap corners will now look as shown in 3. Having completed the folds, stitch all sides a little from the edge of the hem. Attach burlap to lacing set as for the round design.

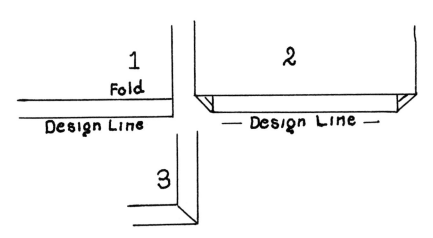

FIG. 14.   Hemming a square-cornered pattern

❧ 6 ❧

Mental Attitude and Posture

This undertaking, making a hooked chair seat, is a *hobby* not *work*. As hobbies are things to do in your spare time, see to it that your regular daily duties are taken care of so that your mind is free to think only of your hooking. Concentration on the subject at hand will then be much easier, better results will be obtained and you will really enjoy your hooking.

Equally important is your position and posture at your frame. Almost any kitchen or dining room chair (except an upholstered one) is suitable if the easel part of the frame can be raised or lowered to suit the chair you are to use. If the frame is not so constructed, regulate the height of your sitting position so that your right arm will be in a comfortable position without having to raise your shoulder to handle your hook. If necessary, bring the chair to the proper height with a cushion or pad.

Sit square with the frame, not sideways. As you hook on either the left or right of the center, move the frame so that this position is maintained. Don't reach any more than is absolutely necessary.

Some of my readers may think these suggestions are a lot of nonsense, but in my Vermont studio I was very careful that these conditions were carried out. The result was that no pupil was ever troubled with backache or shoulder pains from hooking. (Some might come to class with a slight lameness but that was because they had mowed the lawn or weeded their flowerbed. It was not from hooking.) The point I am making is that the wrist and hand should be used, not the upper arm and shoulder.

I am reminded of something my husband, an ardent fly fisherman, told me about the method of teaching that art to beginners. To assure the use of only the forearm and wrist, the upper arm was sometimes strapped to the caster's body so that the shoulder could not be used and perhaps strained. I sometimes thought this method might be helpful in training pupils to hook.

7

Practice Hooking

Even though you have made several rugs, there may be some points that do not entirely satisfy you. Despite my many years in this field, I find I can still learn from other hookers.

The beginner should realize that she should be familiar with certain fundamentals in order to produce an article of which she will be justly proud. If I were to teach an inexperienced pupil, the first lesson would be entirely on the technique of making the loop. This would be followed by hours of practice on the loop before we gave any thought to the design. I have had many pupils who were rather discouraged, at the start, because they were not allowed to make a rose or some other flower at the first lesson, and because they were required to spend an hour of each of three or four subsequent lessons practicing just "that old loop." But later in their courses of instruction, they have all thanked me for obliging them to practice the loop until they automatically made it smoothly and evenly.

First, using the finest cutter head, cut strips of your background material $\frac{3}{32}$ inch wide and 6 inches long. I do not advise a longer strip for practice work, as it will become worn and be wasted. Use a corner of the surplus burlap, outside your design, for practice work.

Hold the strip of material between the thumb and first finger of the left hand, under the burlap. (See Fig. 15.) With the right hand, grasp the hook handle in the palm. (Do not hold it as you would a pen or pencil.) Push the hook through a mesh of the burlap, meeting the wool strip between the thumb and finger of the left hand. (At first, it's quite hard to find that left hand with your hook, but practice makes perfect.)

With the hook, pull the *end* of the wool strip through the burlap. (Always have the ends on top.) Hook through burlap again and pull up a loop of the material. Remove the hook from the loop and, with the left hand, pull the loop down to the height of nap you wish to produce. Continue drawing through loops in each mesh of the burlap and in a straight line about four inches long. This first practice is a sample for a straight-line border. Make all loops as even and close together as possible.

Directly under or above the line just hooked, start a second line going

48

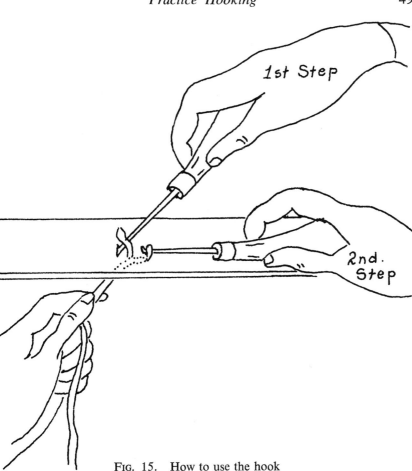

Fig. 15. How to use the hook

into the mesh next to the one previously hooked. With narrow cuttings care must be used to place each loop in each mesh in order to have a good solid nap that will resist accumulation of dirt between the loops.

Continue one row after another, evenly hooked, until you have covered an inch-wide surface. By this time you should have the "feel" of the hook and the left-hand control of the cloth. Always try to avoid snagging the material with the end of the hook when you pull it through the burlap.

BACKGROUND PRACTICE

We will now start practice on hooking background. Just as an aid in training the eye, I suggest using a different color from that used in the band border practice. Start this practice above the band just hooked.

For a smooth background effect, free from any indication of design, I hook in a wavy line. To practice on this, draw a wavy line with a carbon pencil just a bit above the band border just hooked, as shown in Fig. 16.

Be sure this line is "wavy" without any tendency toward a V in either upper or lower curve, as indicated in WRONG above. Make your lines short and uneven as in RIGHT above. If you draw and then hook the lines with V points, you will build up a design that will "stick out like a sore thumb." Such a design would destroy the beauty of the background, whose only purpose in a hooked article is to act as a pleasing but inconspicuous resting place for the design to lie on. Practice hooking several wavy lines until you are able to hook the "wave" without any guiding line.

When you have gained confidence from your practice work, start hooking the chair seat. For your assistance I am giving you a series of simple chair seat designs with suggestions for your colors and methods of hooking.

RIGHT   WRONG

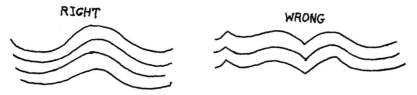

FIG. 16.   Background hooking

❧ 8 ❧

Suggested Colors and Instruction for Hooking Chair Seat Design No. 54

We will first take the design on your frame, No. 54 (Fig. 17).

Outside border. Use first five shades (number one shade being the lightest) of the Allen swatch (see Chapter 3), Aqua Blue or wool that you have dyed in five shades of Aqua Blue. Start the double border by hooking the outside line, next to the binding, with the 5th (or darkest) shade. Next to this dark border edge, hook one row of the 4th shade and continue the rows to the next line of double border with the 3rd, 2nd and 1st shades.

Next, hook one row of Dark Maroon, filling in to inside line with 5th shade of Aqua Blue.

Note. You will observe through the course of this book that the only outlining I use is in geometrics, orientals and borders.

Heart design A. For this particular heart use five graduated shades of American Beauty, omitting the lightest shade. Start hooking on the inside line at point 1, with darkest shade, which in the swatch is Shade 6, follow left-hand line to center point of heart. Repeat outline on same inside line opposite beginning at point 1 as before.

Next to this dark line hook one row of Shade 5, then Shade 4, then Shade 3, finishing on the outside line of the heart with Shade 2. Be sure to start each line of color at point 1, hooking first to the left, then to the right. This will give a very attractive "mitered" effect.

Heart design B. Using Allen swatch, Purple, hook this heart in exactly the same manner as Design A.

Heart design C. Using Aqua Blue swatch, hook this heart in exactly the same manner as Designs A and B.

Heart D will be Purple, E will be American Beauty and F Aqua Blue.

Long pointed ovals where hearts cross each other, fill with Light Gold, lengthwise hooking.

Background. I have used Light Beige to good advantage. Hook the background in wavy lines as shown in Fig. 16. It is surprising to find what an

51

Dark Maroon

FIG. 17.   Chair Seat Design No. 54

attractive chair seat can be made with a simple geometric design by the proper selection of colors. Try out different combinations and you may marvel at the results.

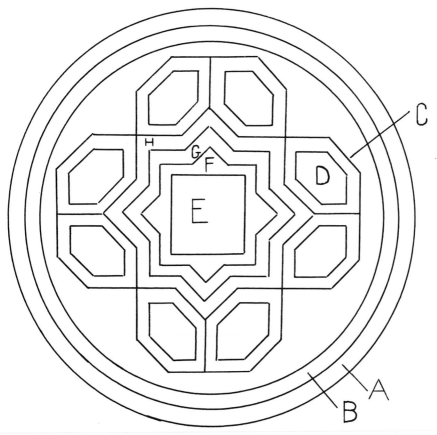

❦ 9 ❧

Suggested Colors and Instruction for Hooking Chair Seat Design No. 51

Here is another geometric you will enjoy hooking. Follow general hooking instructions given for Chair Seat No. 54.

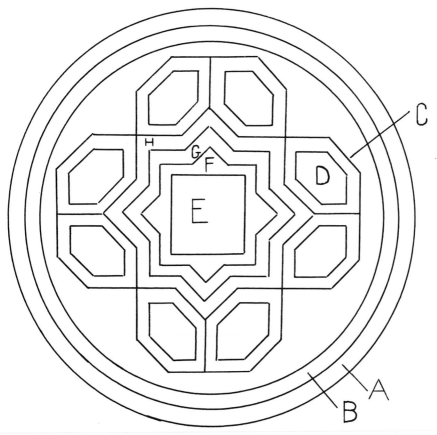

Fig. 18.   Chair Seat Design No. 51

53

Outside border band, A. Allen swatch, Spice Brown, first 5 shades.

Inside border band, B. Allen swatch, Leaf Green, first 5 shades.

Outline figure C with medium shade Leaf Green. Inner line with lightest shade Spice Brown. Fill with other four shades of Spice Brown, ending next to Green line with darkest, mitering the corners as explained in directions for "Heart Design A," Chapter 8.

Center, D. Fill center with 3rd shade of Purple, hooking lengthwise of the figure. Repeat in other seven figures of this shape.

Center square, E. Outline outside line with Gold. Fill with 3rd shade Leaf Green.

First band outside of square, F. Use 5 shades of Spice Brown, starting with dark shade next to Gold outline of square, mitering the corners.

Second band, G. Use 5 shades of Leaf Green, starting with dark shade next to light shade of Spice Brown.

Third band, H. Use 5 shades of Purple, starting with dark shade next to light shade of Leaf Green.

Background. Light Beige.

❧ 10 ☙

Suggested Colors and Instruction for Hooking Miss Muffet Chair Seat Design No. 3

You should now be ready for a more difficult design than a geometric. Here is one of my floral chair-seat designs to test your hooking ability and start you off on real shading.

FIG. 19.   Chair Seat Design No. 3, "Miss Muffet"

55

It is wise to decide what your background color is to be before hooking the design of a floral pattern. I suggest a Dusty White.

BORDER

For the border color, use five shades of Allen swatch Aqua Blue, omitting the lightest shade, 1. (Later we will bring the Aqua Blue into the leaves and spots in the bouquet.) If you have already used some of these lovely shades in your living room, the chair seat will blend with the other colors in the room.

Start the outside line of the border, next to the binding, with the 6th or darkest shade of Aqua Blue. Next to this dark border edge, hook a row of the 5th shade and continue the rows to the inside line of border with 4th, 3rd and 2nd shades.

ROSE LEAF

In the course of instruction from here on, you will find I have used the terms "fingering in" and "directional hooking." Fingering in is to hook a shade in between the rows of the shade previously hooked to produce a subtle flow of color rather than an abrupt change. Only a few loops in this manner are necessary to break up a sharp line of color.

Directional hooking is indicated on the drawings by the shading lines which, you will note, do not go around and around a leaf or petal but from the vein of a leaf *out* toward the edge or *in* from the edge toward the vein. The same is true on most petals.

We will first give our attention to the rose leaf, 1 in Fig. 19. First hook the veins with tiny-checked material (perhaps Dark Red and Green) or Paisley.

For the leaf, use Allen swatch, Leaf Green, or material dyed in six shades with regular Green dye. Beginning on center vein, hook the shadow

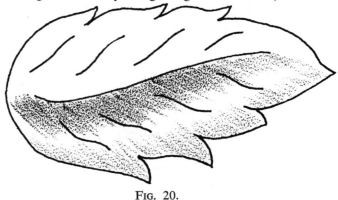

FIG. 20.

A (shown in Fig. 20), using darkest shade at base of leaf and next darkest shade toward the tip, hooking from center vein out.

Then, beginning at the outside edge of leaf, hook the lesser shadow B toward the center, using 3rd light shade at base and 2nd light shade toward the tip.

Fill in C, the space between A and B, with similar diagonal rows of 5th shade at base and fourth shade toward tip. In filling the space, finger the rows into the ones previously hooked, to produce a smooth graduation of color.

Repeat these instructions on all other leaves of the design, varying the color of Greens, if you wish. Olive Green, Grey Green and Yellow Green work in together nicely, and the Aqua Blue shades would be suitable for the leaf just above the pansy.

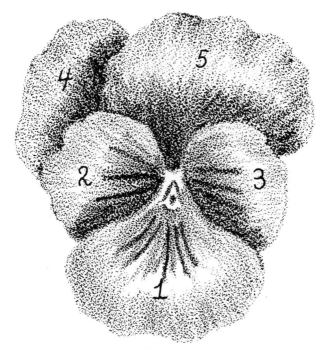

Fig. 21.

PANSY
(2 in Fig. 19)

(*Note:* In the Stratton method, no flower petal is outlined. Remember, too, that when shade numbers are given, the lightest shade is Shade 1, next light, Shade 2, and so on to the darkest shade, Shade 6.)

First Step. Hook the center "nose" and "lips" with White, making the dot Dark Green. This dark dot indicates a hole deep into the pansy stem and gives expression to the flower.

Second Step. Petal 1. Hook four or five curved lines in Yellow at nose and lips, as indicated. Do not outline the petal edge.

Third Step. Hook directionally (from edge toward center), with 2nd light shade of the six graduated shades chosen.

Fourth Step. Hook center of petal with lightest shade.

Fifth Step. Hook your darkest shade up between Yellow lines.

Sixth Step. Hook 2nd dark shade between those just hooked and graduate to the center highlight, and from the 2nd light edge to the highlight, fingering in each shade for perfect graduation.

Seventh Step. Hook petals 2, 3, 4, and 5 in similar manner, noting shadows where any petal disappears behind another one. . . .

MORNING GLORY
(3 in drawing)

A. Hook each small leaf with Green, shading as described under *Rose Leaf.*

B. Flower tube. Use Off White and delicate Green, shadowing the lower part and sides of tube with delicate Pink. In the center front of the tube place your highlight with lightest shade of Off White.

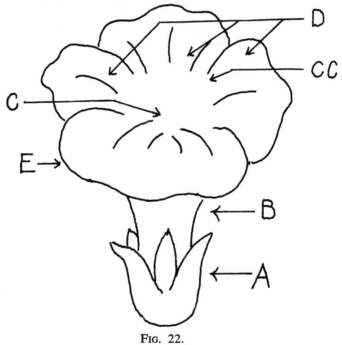

FIG. 22.

C. Center. You are now going to make the inside of the throat. Starting at point shown by arrow, use Muted Old Gold graduating up to the top of the throat (CC) with palest Yellow White.

D. For this area use Allen swatch Blue, fingering into the Yellow-White area with palest Blue shade and graduating out to edge of petal, ending with 4th dark shade of Blue.

E. Front petal. Hook lower edge of front petal with short rows of 2nd light shade of Blue in direction shown.

Then, beginning at top of front petal, hook short rows of 2nd light shade of Blue in direction shown. Fill space between with 1st shade of Blue, fingering into both rows of 2nd light just completed. Using the light shade all across the center of this front petal produces the "roll" you desire.

ROSE
(4 in Fig. 19)

FIG. 23.

The line A to A in Fig. 24 represents the "bowl shape" of the rose petals as they join the drooping petals. Both continue underneath to the stem, out of sight. Naturally, the base of the bowl must be the darkest shade.

The line A to A represents the "bowl shape" of the Rose petals as they join the drooping petals and both continue underneath to the stem, out of sight. Naturally the base of the Bowl must be the darkest shade.

So, for a red rose, hook one row on line A to A with Shade 6 of Allen swatch, American Beauty. Next, for shadow (B) use Shade 5 in short rows of directional hooking. For highlight (C) hook short rows of Shade 1 through center of petal as indicated. Then, working from upper edge of petal (D) toward highlight, use Shade 2 in short rows of directional hooking, fingering into the highlight. Next, for area (E), between base shadow (B) and highlight (C), use Shade 4 next to 5, then Shades 3 and 2 in order, fingering into each other.

The left-hand petal, just hooked, laps over the right-hand petal so hook shadow (F) as indicated, with Shade 4 in short directional rows. Then repeat, *in same order* as you hooked the first petal.

On all other petals follow the same procedure, being sure to note where shadows and highlights are indicated on the drawing. Complete *one* petal at a time.

For unopened center petals (G) use mixture of Green, Brown and Yellow.

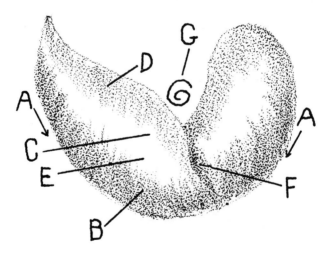

Fig. 24. Rose petals

FIG. 25.   Design No. 378, "Field Scroll," hooked by Mrs. Lavina Laird, Mont-pelier, Vermont

FIG. 26. Design No. 289, "Strawberry Ringleaf," hooked by Mrs. Charles Turner, Schenectady, New York

FIG. 27. Four chair-seat designs, hooked by Mrs. Edith Kelsey, Westfield, Massachusetts

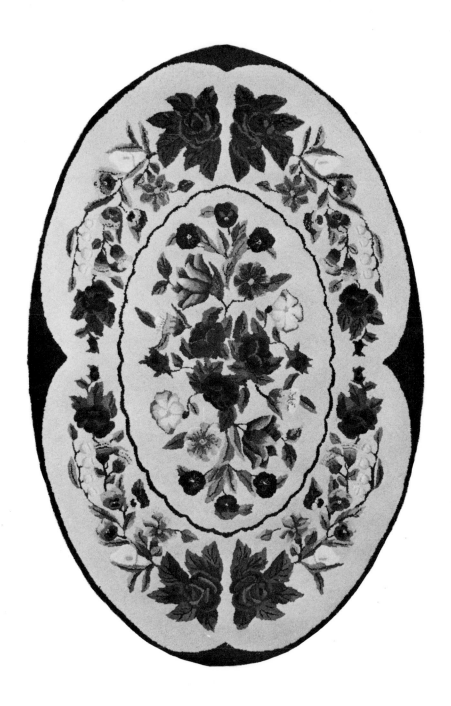

FIG. 28.   Design No. 405, "Charlgard," hooked by Mrs. Guy Jamieson, Millinocket, Maine

PLATE I

Design No. 444, "Harmony."
Perfection hooking by Mrs. Delta Harmon,
Longmeadow, Massachusetts.

PLATE II

Design No. 234, "Vermont Fireplace Rug,"
hooked by Mrs. Ella Goodrich,
Greenfield, Massachusetts.
Delightful selection of colors.

PLATE III

Design No. 262, "Antoinette's Bridal Rug,"
hooked by Mrs. Mildred Millhouse,
West Hartford, Connecticut.
An exceptional background of Antique Black,
expertly executed.

PLATE IV

Design No. 365, "Roumanian Convent,"
hooked by Mrs. Marie Hutchins,
Springfield, Massachusetts.

PLATE V

Design No. 235, "Persian Oriental,"
hooked by Miss Frieda Powers,
Bernardston, Massachusetts.

PLATE VI

Frost Design No. 108, "Turkish Oriental,"
hooked by Mrs. Blanche Godfrey,
Gardner, Massachusetts.

PLATE VII

Design No. 249, "Priscilla Pansies,"
hooked by Mrs. Alice Croteau,
Northampton, Massachusetts.

PLATE VIII

Design No. 435, "Summer Bloom,"
hooked by Mrs. Florence Peck,
Newtown, Connecticut.
A beautiful rug, nicely made.

11

Instruction for Hooking Leaves

Material for fronds, five shades of Allen swatch Grey Green or Olive Green. The directions given apply to any of my fern designs.

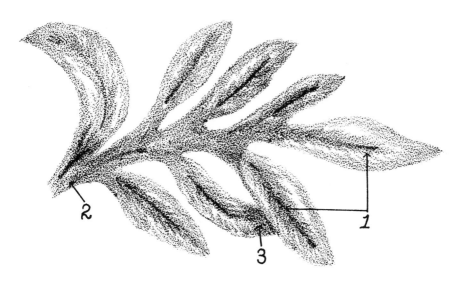

FIG. 29.   Fern

First, hook the veins (1) with Green and Brown pin-check mixture. Then, at base of fern (2) use 4th and 5th shades, starting on lower part of stem at right of vein, hooking directionally as illustrated. Do not hook a straight line next to vein as that would flatten the fern as though it were pressed. Let us have some contour.

Hook the lower right-hand frond first using three light shades. Hook lightest shade only at the point and part way down the upper side. (Never have a light line following all around a frond or leaf edge.) Continue

81

hooking diagonally on the narrow part of stem to the second frond. Notice that the point of this second frond (3) is tucked under the third frond. Hook your 3rd shade a small amount, for shadow at the spot where it passes under, using same diagonal hooking as given in previous lessons and illustrated here. Repeat on each of the remaining fronds to the last one on left-hand side. Notice its curve. Use first three shades on upper part or hump of the frond. The lower side of this frond is concave; therefore it must be shadowed. Visualize by bending your index finger in an arc and studying its shape, shadows and highlight. On the inside of the finger you want shadows and the top of your bent finger must have light shades graduating to the dark.

Fɪɢ. 30. Design No. 461, "Fern Fronds"

Follow directional hooking lines illustrated and *do not outline*.

The directions given above apply to any of my fern designs. Fig. 30 is from my pattern No. 461, "Fern Fronds," size 19 x 37 inches. This design is available in No. 461-A, 25 x 37 inches or can be made larger as desired by adding strips of six-inch blocks.

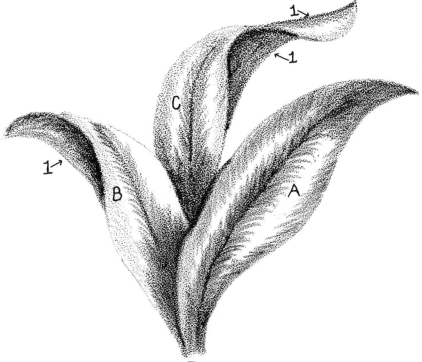

FIG. 31.

TULIP LEAVES

You will notice that Fig. 31 includes a plain leaf (A), a single turnover (B), and a double turnover (C).

First, hook the veins in all three leaves. Then, for balance of leaf (A), follow directions given for leaves in chair seat No. 3, Chapter 10, using the family of Green most pleasing to you.

Next, hook turnover areas marked 1, in directional hooking, using second light shade as indicated, graduating to lightest on the edges of rollovers. Never outline a rollover.

Complete leaves B and C as you hooked leaf A. Watch your shadows, highlights, and directional hooking.

Rose Leaves

The rose leaves in Fig. 32 are like the tulip leaves except for their shape. The flat leaf A is hooked like any flat leaf and leaf B is a turnover.

Follow shadows and highlights and directional hooking lines. Do not outline. Always apply the "leaf" directions, already given, to any leaf formation.

Fɪɢ. 33.

OAK LEAVES

Fig. 33 shows two oak leaves, different in formation from other leaves previously shown, but the method of hooking is the same. Because of the formation, you must use slightly different shading, as indicated on the drawing. Also note that Leaf A lies on Leaf B. *Do not outline.*

FIG. 34.

SILVER-MAPLE LEAF

Try your luck at shading the silver-maple leaf in Fig. 34. See how easy it will be to hook it when you find it in a rug pattern.

F<small>IG</small>. 35.   Design No. 261, "Indian Summer," hooked by Mrs. Ella Goodrich,
Greenfield, Massachusetts

Fɪɢ. 36. Design No. 433, "Hayes Floral." Hooked by Mrs. Roy Thomas, Houlton, Maine

FIG. 37.   Design No. 381, "Gorgeous," hooked by Mrs. Leo Spain, Houlton, Maine

Fig. 38.   Design No. 388, "Woodpeckers," hooked by the author

12

Instruction for Hooking Flowers

FIG. 39.

DAISY

For the daisy in Fig. 39, hook the center disk (1) in directional lines, using the colors of the type of daisy you have chosen. Hook the "rays," as daisy petals are called, following directional lines and areas of shadows and highlights. To make any drooping petal "curve," you should shadow the tip, working up into the lighter shades on the hump.

Sometimes the colors used for the disk are Yellow to Cream, or Brown to Golden, or others. I am not giving you the shades of color to use in each spot since you are now in an advanced stage of hooking and able to use your own reasoning.

Dogwood

For center of dogwood, Fig. 40, use tweeds of plain Greens, shadow with Dark Greens imitating a stiff "thorny" effect.

Start flower with petal 1. Where petal joins center, 2, use three shades of Medium Dark Grey. For indentation at tip of petal use Medium Light Reddish Brown shades. Hook edge of petal with second light shade, with White through the center of the petal. Repeat on other petals. Watch directional lines for hooking, and do not outline.

If you wish a pink dogwood, follow same directions with shades of **Pink**.

Fɪɢ. 40.

Dahlia

Make center of dahlia, Fig. 41, similar to dogwood. Hook petals also similar to the dogwood but smaller. Follow shadows and highlights as illustrated, hooking on directional lines. Always reason "why" your shadow is here and highlight there. *Do not outline your petals.*

FIG. 41.

A Simple Rose Form

The rose in Fig. 42 is something for you to play with. No directions are given for hooking it. Test the knowledge you have acquired by taking a tracing of the design, drawing it on some odd end of burlap and hooking it without reference to directions for other rose forms. Use your own ideas on the shadows and highlights. Then check with the first directions for a rose (see Figs. 23 and 24), and make such corrections as seem necessary. This will help you to remember the details.

I know you will have fun doing it. This is the method I have always used in my classes to help pupils to increase the knowledge they have acquired.

FIG. 42.

Rose with Rollover Petals

The only general difference between the Rose in Fig. 43 and others for which directions for hooking have been given are the "turnover" or "rollover" petals numbers 1, 2, 3, 4 and 5 as shown. Hook rollovers first, beginning with 1, then 2, 3 and 4, saving 5 for last as both ends pass under the petals on each side, therefore this 5 petal requires slightly more shading than the others.

Follow directional hooking lines using the darker shades where shadows are indicated and lighter shades for the highlights.

Hook the base of petals 1 and 2 as indicated, remembering that the line A to A represents the "bowl shape" of the rose petals as they join the drooping petals and both continue underneath to the stem, out of sight. Naturally the base of the bowl must be the darkest shade.

So, to establish this darkest part of the rose and the line where your up-and-down directional lines begin, hook one line A to A with your darkest shade.

For remaining petals follow directions given for the rose on Chair Seat No. 3, Chapter 10.

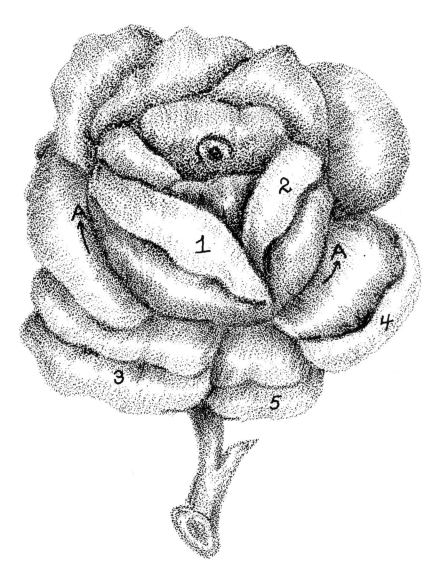

FIG. 43.

CHRYSANTHEMUM

In hooking the Chrysanthemum (Fig. 44), the colors may be White through Yellow to Bronzy Gold or Grey to White, six Shades.

Hook base of petals between A and A with single line of darkest shade. Hook 2nd and 3rd dark shades at base of petal 1, hooking diagonally from line A up toward center of petal. Hook narrow edge with 2nd light, lightest for highlight. Graduate the shades down into the shadow.

Repeat same direction on petals 2 to 6.

You now know where shadows and highlights should be; follow drawing on all other petals. Note that the drooping petals are hooked exactly like the ones first completed, except that your direction is *down* from line A instead of up.

Hook the turnovers on petals (7) first, then the shadow back of the roll.

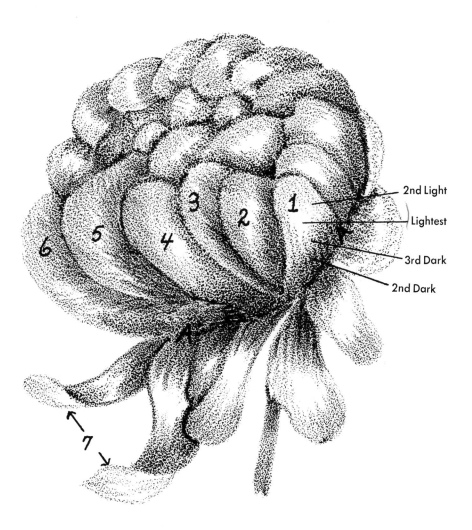

2nd Light

Lightest

3rd Dark

2nd Dark

FIG. 44.

POPPY

The poppy in Fig. 45 has two "rollover" petals similar to the single rollover of the calla lily (see page 109). Hook these rollovers first, using two lightest shades on edges at 1, then with lightest shade through middle area 2. Shadow two lower front petals 3, under rollover as illustrated. Side petals 4, shadow as shown, light on the roll, darker on the edge. Inside petals 5, back of rollover, use four darkest shades, working each petal as directed for other flowers, following directional lines. Do not outline.

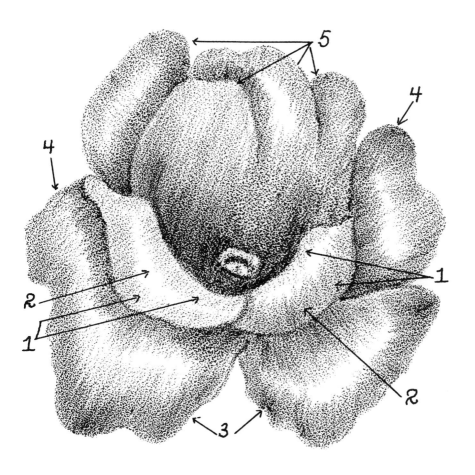

Single French Rose

Here again, in Fig. 46, for the base of the "cup" shape, use three dark shades in directional lines according to instructions for double rose (Fig. 43), hooking three front petals first. For inside of rose use proper shades in shadows and highlights as shown on the drawing. Do not outline the petals. Hook seeds in center with mixtures, Green, Brown or Gold.

FIG. 46.

Morning Glory

For the morning glory, Fig. 47, hook front rollover first using 2nd light from B to B. Hook 2nd light from A to A on lower edge of rollover. Use lightest shade up and down through center of roll, meshing into both edges of the 2nd light.

Notice that the lightest shade in center of roll indicates the roll curve or bulge of the petal.

Hook Center (C) using faded Olive Green. Hook area above with 4th and 3rd light following directional lines and meshing into the Olive Green.

All around outer edge of flower use 2nd light, from edge toward high-light. Do not outline.

Hook highlight with lightest shade, meshing into 2nd light on edge, again producing the "roll" or shape of the flower. Hook tube as shown.

For leaf, apply instruction on leaves, Chapter 12.

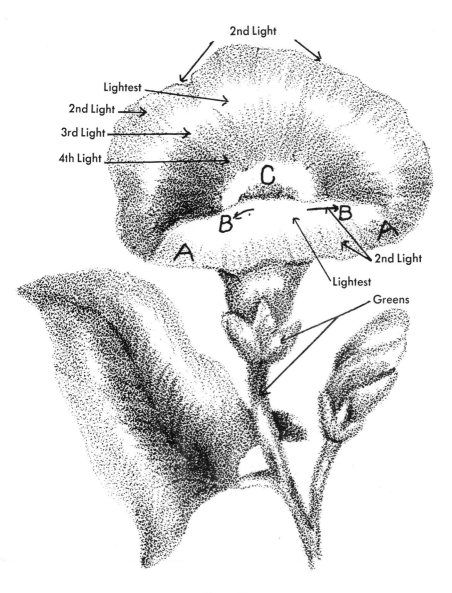

FIG. 47.

CALLA LILY

In making a calla lily (see Fig. 48) I always hook the rollover first, using pure White at 1 in directional hooking as illustrated. Never outline a rollover. On upper and lower edges use 2nd light Grey shade, hooking directionally as illustrated at 2. Do not hook from "end to end."

For the spadix, 3, use Yellow shadowed with Old Gold. In area 4, shadow with three deepest shades of Grey, in direction shown. (This shadow is on the inside of the flower, on its *back* wall.)

Above, on the roll of this part of the flower, at arrow 5, hook a band of White. This is your highlight, making the back roll and giving contour.

At outside edge 6, use 2nd light all across, fingering into the White. Do not outline this upper petal.

Next, we will hook the tube of the lily. Visualize this as a round tube; therefore, we hook a shadow along each side and small amount on the base, working lengthwise of the tube. Also, shadow *under* the rollover. White and Grey White through the up and down of the center of the tube. This is the highlight that indicates the roundness of the tube. At each step of hooking a calla lily or other kinds of lilies follow the directional lines I have indicated. Note that you have done no outlining so this flower will lie *on* the background instead of being imbedded *in* it.

Calla lilies may also be hooked in Yellow with equally pleasing results.

Hook calla leaf, using directions given for first leaf, Chapter 11.

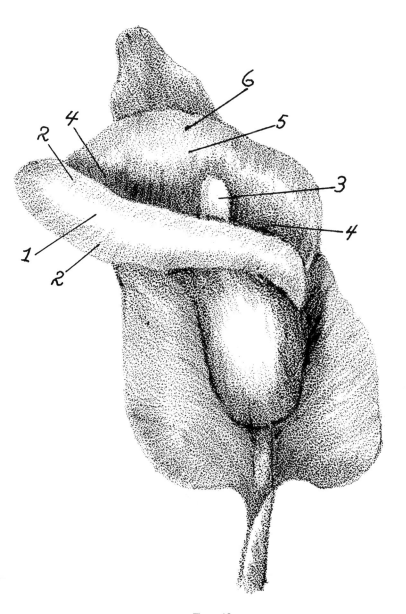

Fig. 48.

DAFFODIL

Hook the daffodil in Fig. 49 as follows:

First, hook roll (A) with 2nd light as shown with the lightest through center. Hook pistil with two shades of Olive Green. Next, hook area back of the pistil with 2nd and 3rd dark, 2nd light and lightest as shown, always following the directional lines, meshing together, and do not outline. Hook base of tube with 3rd and 2nd dark, hook upper part under the roll with 2nd dark and lightest through center.

Petal (1). 2nd light around edge, lightest for highlight. Second and 3rd dark for shadows under the bowl. Graduate your shades between. Repeat on other petals as shown in Fig. 49.

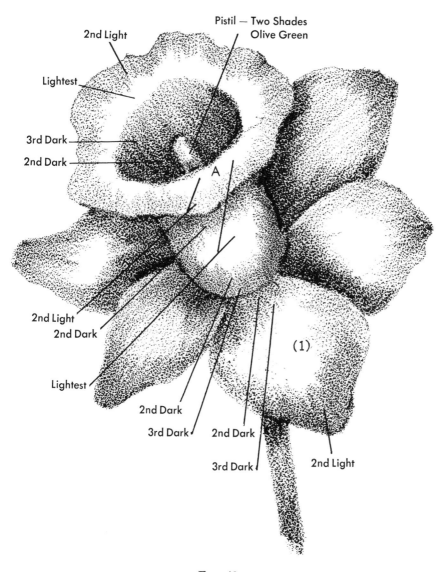

2nd Light

Pistil — Two Shades
Olive Green

Lightest

3rd Dark

2nd Dark

A

2nd Light
2nd Dark

Lightest

2nd Dark

3rd Dark

2nd Dark

3rd Dark

2nd Light

(1)

FIG. 49.

A Common Type of Lily

The lily in Fig. 50 has a tube for a base and petals hanging over it, similar to the morning glory, petunia, calla lily, etc.

Instructions given previously apply to hooking this lily. The inside dark center is a hole down into the tube. Dark shadow lines, 1, flow down into the tube.

On edges and tips of pointed petals use 2nd and 3rd light shades with palest shade through the petal centers for highlights.

When petal tips turn over on this or any similar figure, hook them before making the rest of the petal. On the two turnover tips of petals in this lily use two lightest shades as indicated in the drawing. Please note that petal 2 turns under while petal 3 turns up, therefore the light and next light are in opposite positions.

Follow the shadows and directional lines of the Stratton method. Do not outline.

This lily is beautiful in Red Grape or Purple or burnt shades of Yellow.

Fig. 50.

ROYAL LILY

For the lily in Fig. 51, as shown in previous directions, hook first the front rollover petal (1), applying the instructions for calla lily. The petal is the same except for the shape.

Next, hook left-hand petal (2), noting that this is also a petal that "rolls" toward you from under the side of petal 1. Therefore, watch your shadows.

Next, hook petal 3, another rollover, noting that 3A area is the back side of the petal 3 so of course must be shaded to indicate this. Then, hook the tube (4) as instructed on other tube flowers.

Note: Petals 5, 6 and 7 are the "back" petals of the lily. Note location of shadows.

Stamens, in center, hook in Brown with Pale Green stems.

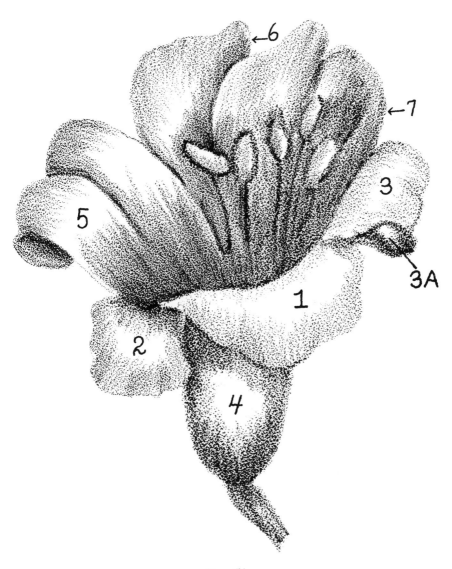

Fig. 51.

ORCHID

There are many types of orchids, from the common wild lady's slipper to the beautful hybrid variety shown in Fig. 52.

The areas 1 are hooked exactly as you were shown for the daffodil, except that the edge of the bowl petals on the orchid are wavy. The same difference occurs on the large petals (2).

Use your choice of orchid colors, following directional hooking lines for shadows and highlights. *Do not outline.*

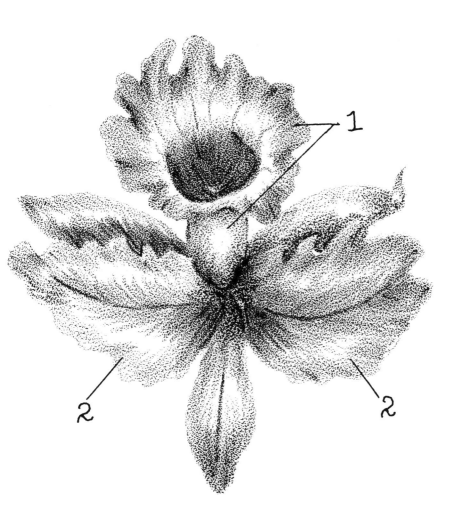

FIG. 52.

IRIS

The iris shown in Fig. 53 is of the bearded variety with three sepals, 2, and 3 bearded at 1, three petals, 4, 5, 6, and a single pistil, 8.

Use any color you wish, six or eight closely graduated shades. Follow directional lines as illustrated, using care with highlights and shadows. First, hook the three beards, numbers 1, using Yellow shadowed with Gold. Next, hook lower large sepal, 2, following directional lines. (A beautiful colored picture of an iris will assist you in applying my treatment of shadows and highlights.) Then, hook sepals 3 following illustration.

Petal 4 follows, and then petal 5, noting the shadow where petal 4 laps over the 5th petal. Small area, 6, is the tip of the back petal whose center base shows at area 7. The tip, being back of the two upper petals, requires careful shading. For center, 7, use shades of color shown in the picture you have chosen as a guide. The shape of this area varies in different types of iris. Hook pistil, 8, as indicated in your colored picture.

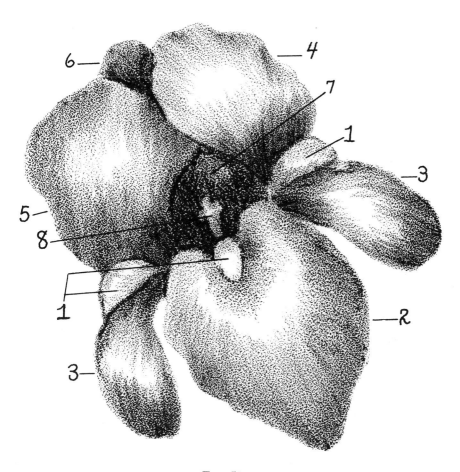

FIG. 53.

TULIP

To hook the tulip shown in Fig. 54, follow instruction given in Chapter 10, where the morning glory is discussed. Choose your favorite colors. I feel strongly that each hooker should be permitted to express her own taste.

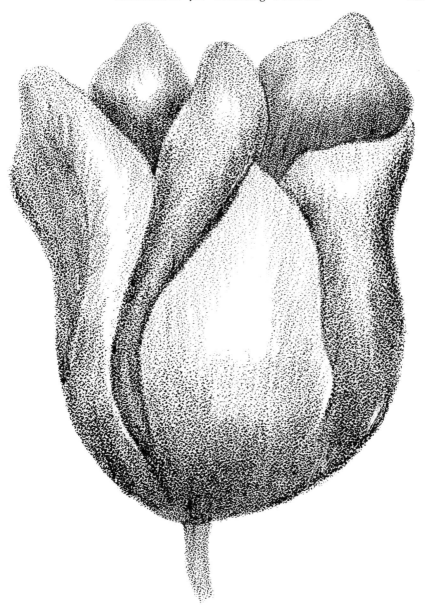

Fig. 54.

An Unusual Darwin Tulip

For the tulip shown in Fig. 55, hook the rolls of petals 1 and 2 first, following directional lines and shades as shown.

Next, hook base of petals 1 and 2 as indicated. Through the center of petal 3, 4, hook diagonally with 2nd, 3rd and 4th dark shades, with lightest for highlight, as shown.

For petals 5, 6 and 7, follow as shown on drawing.

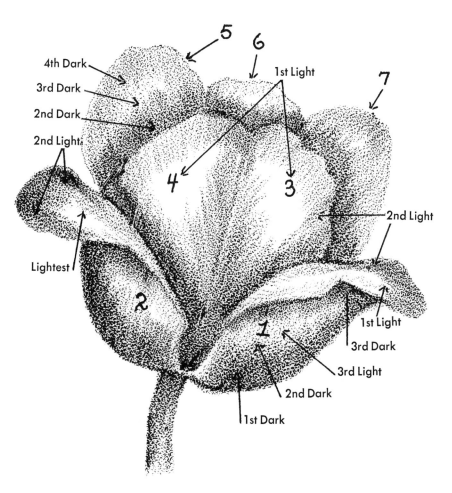

FIG. 55.

Fig. 56.   Design No. 294, "Petals and Plumes," hooked by Mrs. Marion La-
reau, Turners Falls, Massachusetts

Fig. 57. Design No. 279, "Parade of Roses," hooked by Harold Ransom, Hartford, Connecticut

FIG. 58. Design No. 263, "Maine Cone and Tassel," hooked by Mrs. Genevieve Pont Briand, Northampton, Massachusetts

FIG. 59. Design No. 436, "Doorway Favorite," hooked by Mrs. Charles Turner, Schenectady, New York

13

Instruction for Hooking Scrolls

EASY SCROLL

Five graduated shades of Plum make a very nice colored scroll (see Fig. 60). We usually dye this. Or use Allen swatch Aqua Blue, first five shades.

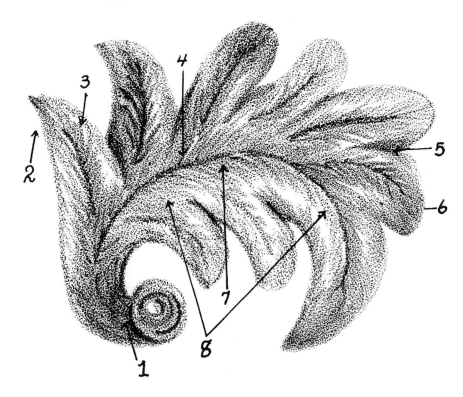

FIG. 60.

Hook veins with Red mixture, keeping it muted. These veins must not be prominent. Use first three shades of Plum, starting at base of scroll (1) just to left of knob, hooking each side diagonally as illustrated.

Hook point (2) next, using lightest shade in area 3 with 2nd light on tips. This will give you a contour and your points will have an effect of bending, leaving the hump of the curve in the light. Continue shadows along the upper side of center vein (4) as illustrated, always hooking directional lines until you reach the sixth point.

Notice this sixth point is less pointed and less out in the light. Use 2nd light of your Plum for highlight and 3rd light on edge, hooking shadow at 5. You ask "Why the shadow?" Because the edge is tucked back of the preceding point.

Now the Aqua Blue is going to be used on the main center point and the two points inside the scroll. This shows you how to develop two colors in one scroll. In area 7 on lower side of center vein, hook your Plum, three darker shades or shades numbers 3, 4 and 5, from the main vein out, as before ending unevenly at areas 8 ready to finger in the Aqua Blue.

Hook 3rd and 4th shades of Aqua Blue down between 3rd shade of Plum which is waiting for these Aqua Blue tips. You must always use the same color value shade of another color when fingering the shades together. In oil painting we would use the deeper Aqua Blue on our brush and with a brush stroke down into the Plum we would cause a perfect blend.

Caution: Watch out that the fingering-in of the two colors is sufficiently deep to prevent a definite "cross line" between the two colors. Follow directional hooking lines on all points as illustrated.

Hook the circle at end of scroll with Shades 4 and 5 of Aqua Blue, hooking circularly starting with the lightest on the outside following with Shade 4 and ending in center with Shade 5. I seldom use a contrast color all around a scroll, both top and bottom of the design. I was taught that the contrasting color in scrolls were a trimming or decoration added to the general plan. If we used Aqua Blue around each point it would be as bad as overloading your blouse with trimming of an opposite color.

This Aqua Blue on Pattern No. 458, Scroll Parade, if used on the "inside" of all scrolls around the rug, will produce a gorgeous "new look" to your rug. Other color combinations may be planned by you with equal success if you follow the Stratton directions.

LEAF-TYPE SCROLL

In hooking the scroll shown in Fig. 61, follow instructions for hooking scrolls on preceding pages. All scrolls are executed in the same manner but with varied directional hooking, depending upon the formation or shape of the scroll, and with different colors.

FIG. 61.

Suggested colors for this are, Leaf Green, Off White to Brown, (light Beige shades), Mulberry, Aqua Blue, Strawberry and Old Rose dyed materials, Bronze Gold to Cream, Grey Blues, Deep Silver Grey to White and many others. Use one color for the whole scroll, or make combinations as desired and as explained in previous lesson.

Frost Scroll

The scroll in Fig. 62 appears in the borders of several of the Frost designs. It was probably taken from the carving on some old piece of furniture, clock or other antique article.

As some hookers have wondered just how to hook this scroll, I am giving you these suggestions for the use of graduated shades.

Follow the directional hooking lines, the lights and shades as shown, and I am sure you will be pleased with the result.

The areas 1, 2, 3 and 4 may be in a contrasting color if you wish.

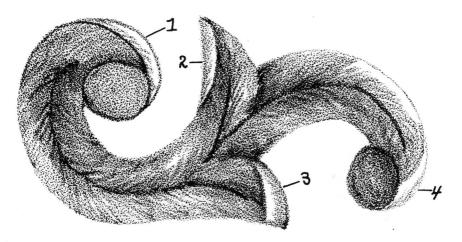

Fig. 62.

14

Instruction for Hooking Borders

ROPE BORDER DESIGN

For the rope border design shown in Fig. 63, follow directional hooking lines with White and four shades of light Silver Grey. This design appears on my patterns "Antique Poppies," No. 209—oval 38 x 52 inches and No. 219—round 39 inches.

This rope border is lovely in Leaf Green to White, Tans to Cream, Old Blues or any colors you may prefer. Of course, your lighter shades are for highlights and the deeper shades for shadows. *Do not outline.*

FIG. 63.

MITERED CORNER BORDER

Any similar border on a rug pattern is a frame enclosing the design just as a picture frame encloses a painting or a photograph. I enjoy hooking such a border to make it *look* like a frame, by mitering the corners. With a carbon pencil draw a diagonal line on each corner of your burlap. Hook *up to* this line from each direction, do not hook *around* the corner.

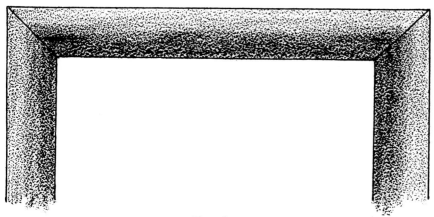

FIG. 64.

And a very attractive border can be made with graduated shades of your chosen color, light on outside, darker on inside, intermediate shades between. Try it and I think you will like it.

15

Instruction for Hooking Stair Carpets

PERSIAN STAIR CARPETS
(Design No. 253)

The Persian stair carpet in Fig. 65 is from a very charming, very old Persian design. It is one of my most popular stair carpets as you have an

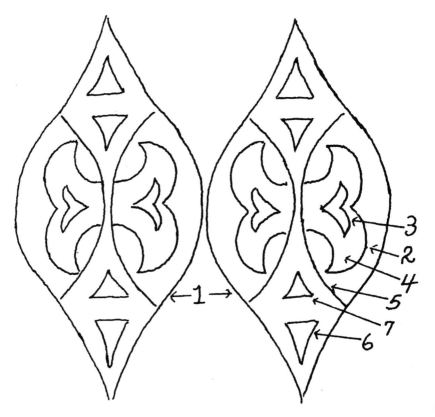

FIG. 65.

opportunity to bring in all Oriental colors you wish to harmonize with your front entrance. If you use Reds be sure they are the Blue Reds and not the Turkish, Yellow Reds. An attractive feature of this design is that it is an "overall" and if extra length is hooked it can be moved up or down when wear on the edges of the treads make it necessary.

Hook outside line (1) of each "pointed oval" motif with Navy Blue. For fan-shaped figure (2) inside pointed oval on right-hand side of design, outline outside edge with Old Gold.

Small figure 3 outline with Gold, fill with 3rd shade of Oriental Blue. Fill in area 4 with 4th shade of Persian Rose Red.

Outline the inside border of oval (5) with Aqua Blue. Repeat in left-hand oval.

For small triangle *in* lower peak (6), outline one line of Old Gold then a second line of Navy Blue, filling center with medium shade of Royal Blue.

Small triangle (7), outline with Medium Blue and Gold, and fill in with third shade of Purple.

Backgrounds may be planned in any way you wish. Same all over or ovals in one shade and pointed corner area in another. The color combinations given above repeat in all other units, which you will note are interlocking. This design is most attractive in any Persian Oriental combinations. It is fun sometimes to pin on your burlap various colors you would enjoy until you find a combination that best suits you and your home. I am always careful to use the correct quantity of light or dark to prevent too pale or too dark an effect. Try for a correct balance of the two.

STAIR CARPET, "ABE LINCOLN'S FANCY"
(Design No. 252, 27 inches wide)

By special request, this design was copied from an authentic illustration of the wallpaper in Abe Lincoln's dining room. It is geometric in form with a strong indication of Turkish Oriental art. Suggested colors are indicated in Figs. 66 and 67. Fig. 66 shows the border design. Fig. 67 shows the motif which runs through the center. Fig. 67 shows the completed carpet, hooked by Mrs. C. L. Montgomery of West Rutland, Vermont, under instruction from Mrs. Nellie S. Paul of Pittsford, Vermont. The wallpaper of Mrs. Montgomery's hall is an antique design with beautiful coloring, and Mrs. Montgomery brought these colors into her stair carpet with excellent results.

For the center motif, she chose Garnet Red with Light Gold (buff) each side. A bit of Black and Pale Green were used each side of the Garnet Red. Borders are Black. Red, Gold, White and Pale Green were used in the motifs. Background is Light Grey.

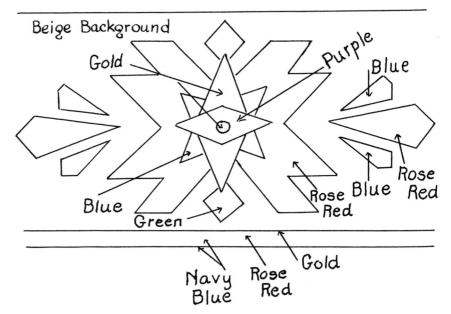

Beige Background

Gold

Purple

Blue

Blue

Green

Rose
Red

Blue

Rose
Red

Navy
Blue

Rose
Red

Gold

FIG. 66.   Border design of "Abe Lincoln's Fancy"

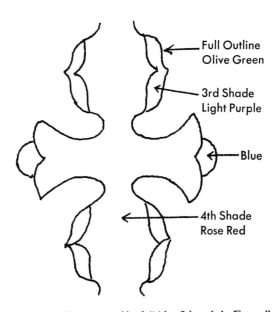

Full Outline
Olive Green

3rd Shade
Light Purple

Blue

4th Shade
Rose Red

FIG. 67.   Center motif of "Abe Lincoln's Fancy"

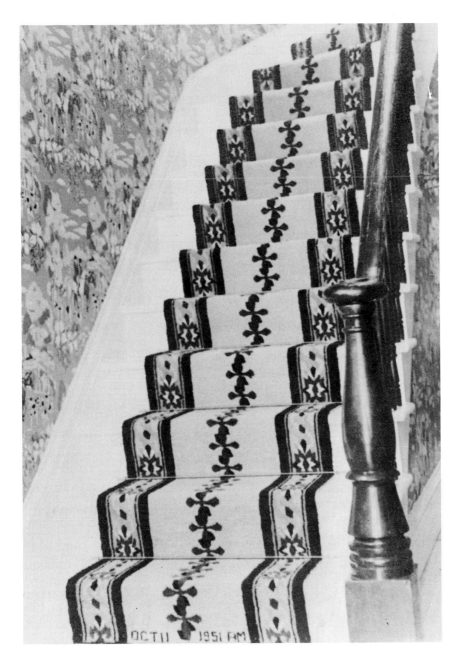

FIG. 68. Design No. 252, "Abe Lincoln's Fancy," hooked by Mrs. C. L. Montgomery, West Rutland, Vermont

FIG. 69.

STAIR CARPET DESIGN NO. 2, "ROSE SPRAY"
(10-inch tread, 8-inch riser)

Choose the colors you desire for the rose spray and follow instructions for roses in Chapters 10 and 12. Bring in some of the same colors and shades in the "hit-or-miss" tread.

FIG. 70.

SCENIC STAIR CARPET, NOS. 3-3L

Fig. 70 is one of a group of thirteen different scenic Stair Risers (Nos. 3-3L) with "hit-or-miss" treads. The group includes a log cabin, country church, farm scenes, houses, etc. The scenes are also available as pictures to use in those old picture frames that have been cluttering up the attic for so long but which are too good to throw away.

16

Instruction for Hooking Acorns and Pine Cones

ACORNS

If you are hooking an unripe acorn the colors will all be in the Green family. If the acorn is fully ripe the colors will be in the Brown family. For the purpose of this demonstration we will consider the acorns in Fig. 71 to be *half* ripe, thus including both color families.

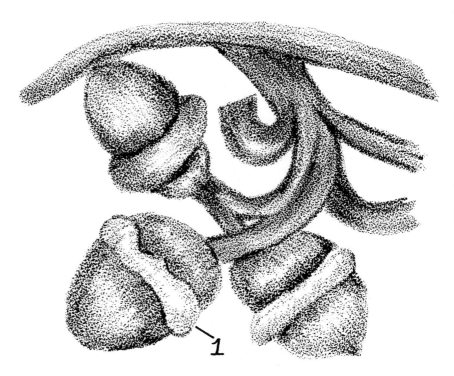

FIG. 71.

FIG. 72.

Cap (1) should be hooked first. Spice Brown is good for this part. Start at the edge of cap (1), hooking on lower and upper edges with the darker shades and the lighter shades through the center, keeping directional lines. For tip of acorn use three shades of Bronze Green, hooking in direction indicated on drawing with the lighter shade for the highlight. Stems may be Browns or Greens as desired. *Do not outline.*

PINE CONE AND TASSEL

Pine cones are composed of small shell-like, woody petals. They grow under each other in layers that form a "cone" around the stem. Usually we hook these in Browns. Some hookers use Mummy Brown.

Start with Shade 1. Shadow as illustrated, graduating to the lightest. I use 2nd light shade on edges. Next, 2 then 3. This starts you on building each small "shell" separately. Follow shadows and highlights as shown, in directional hooking. The outside "shells" should be darker tones than those through the center to give the cone contour. *Do not outline.*

The pine cone and tassel are used in Design No. 263, shown in Fig. 58.

17

Instruction for Hooking Fruits

Because of space limitations it is impossible to give you full and complete directions for hooking each kind of fruit. I could give you a dye formula for each fruit but it might not come out as expected because of the type of material you used, or the shade of White that it was before dyeing.

There are swatches available which have been dyed by experts in this work or, if you have the courage, you could dye your own graduated shades following the colors of any good fruit-tree catalogue.

There are no dye formulas for pears and peaches that would give you the exact colors you need as they are a combination of three or four family colors.

On any round object we paint or hook, we never outline, for that would flatten the outside edge. We curve the sides of all our fruit with hooking lines closer together on outer edge. This will apply to all of my illustrations of fruit.

Remember, the Stratton way is to hook *curved* outside edges, and to use directional hooking wherever the area will permit, plus proper use of graduated shades. This method will produce the rounded shape of any kind of fruit. All fruit colors and shades should be muted, with no one color or shade prominent.

PEAR

Hooking the highlights and shadows of the front part of the pear, Fig. 73, is similar to the manner of hooking the large front petal of a tulip.

Starting at the Base (1) with your Greenish Golden shade, hook as indicated on drawing. Notice the curved directional hooking lines on base and edges. This keeps the rounded shap of the pear. In placing the high-

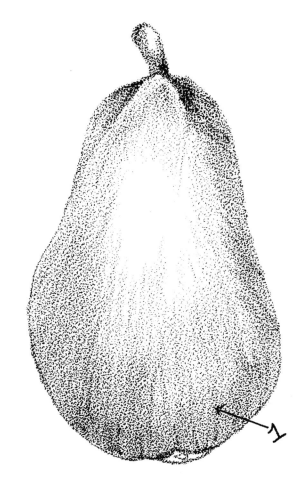

Fig. 73.

light, as indicated, use the graduated shades; finger in to the medium shades already hooked just as you did in front petal of the tulip.

Suggested dyes: Pale Yellow to Antique Brownish Gold, Egyptian Red (clear or overdyed on Yellow).

PEACH

A peach (Fig. 74) is executed in exactly the same manner as a pear except for the colors used and the crease shaded as illustrated. There is no up and down hooking. Some peaches have almost a Mummy Brown to Light Yellow toning.

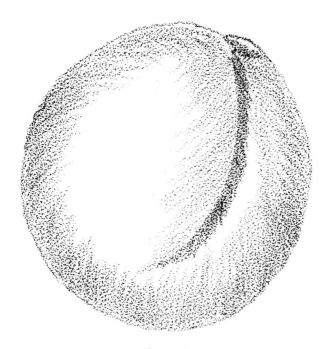

F_{IG}. 74.

GRAPES

Grapes (Fig. 75) may be hooked in several different colors, Purple, White, Cream or Red.

Do not hook around the edge. It will create a flat track around the grape that will destroy any attempt to make it appear round. Start hooking your darker shades at 1, hooking on directional lines toward the highlight shown on the drawing. Continue up the *left* side of the grape. Notice that all lines curve on the sides of the grape to make it round. Next, hook the *right* side. Then hook the highlight using in-between shades going back into the shadows already hooked.

The small grape at the right is partially back of the one just hooked, so hook the *right* side edge in directional hooking, hook the highlight, then hook shadow next to the larger grape graduating your shades into the light. In starting to hook a bunch, apply these directions to the grape nearest to you (A) which is *not* hidden behind any others. Follow with B, C and D to establish where you wish the highlight, to cause the *bulge* of the bunch as a whole. Then hook the other grapes in any order you wish, but remember that some are farther back than others and should be shaded accordingly.

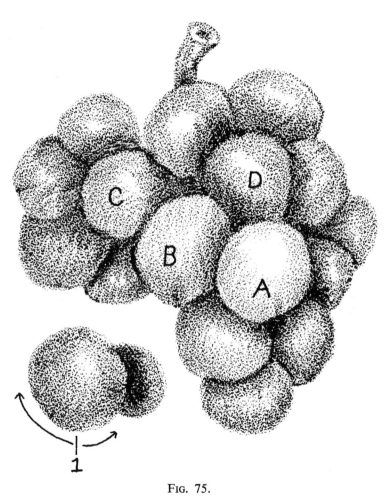

F<small>IG</small>. 75.

CHERRIES

Cherries are hooked just the same as grapes except that the cherries need a little more shadow at the spot where the stem joins the fruit.

Follow the directional hooking lines as indicated in Fig. 76. Perhaps a colored picture of a bunch of cherries will help you with your shading. Do not outline.

In hooking the cherry leaves, apply the directions given for leaves in Chair Seat No. 3. Hook leaf 1 first; then the turnover (2), being careful with the shadows.

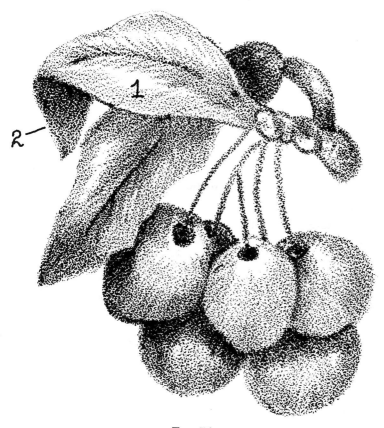

FIG. 76.

Plums

Purple, Red or Green may be used. The size of a plum makes it possible to hook it in the same general manner as shown for the pear and peach.

With the directions for hooking fruit already given, you should be able to exercise your own reasoning and apply what you have learned.

Fig. 77.

STRAWBERRIES

Hook the Green hull in Fig. 78 first. This is just a group of tiny leaves. Study a good picture of a strawberry and note the shadow under the hull. Hook this with Dark Maroon.

Start the strawberry at 1, making short directional hooking lines from edge toward the center. Place highlight as shown. When the berry is completed, hook in single loops of Pale Yellow for the seeds.

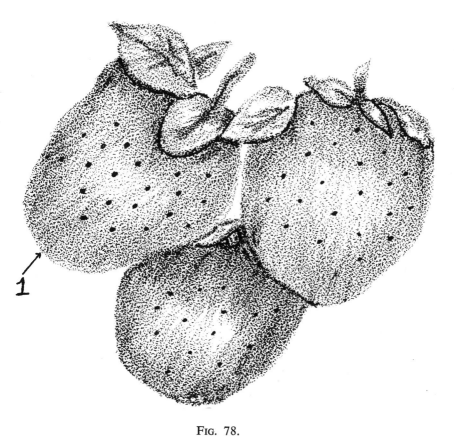

F_{IG}. 78.

APPLE

Start hooking at A, front lower center of apple, Fig. 79. Follow directional lines, working to the right side of the apple to the top. Repeat on left side.

Hook center of the apple, graduating the shades from the dark edge to the light center, placing the highlight where you wish it to be, with the lightest shade. (The same hooking principle is used as shown for the large petal of the tulip.)

At top of apple, note directional lines and shadow around the stem. Hook stem with Green and a little Brown.

A

FIG. 79.

BANANA

Hook stem end 1 first, shading as shown in Fig. 80. Colors: Cream, Pale Yellow and two Brown shades. Follow a colored picture of a banana if you have never painted one. Beginning at 2 hook lower edge with darker shades. Then, beginning at 3, hook the upper edge, hooking lengthwise of the banana, noting where the Brown streaks should be used. If a good picture is not available, use a real banana. Note heavy shadows at each end of the banana.

Fig. 80.

Pineapple

When you hook your first pineapple, I suggest you buy a graduated shade swatch specially dyed for a pineapple to give you an idea of the proper shades of Cream, Faded Yellow and Browns to use. If I were giving you personal instruction on hooking a pineapple, I would show you the wool swatch and a colored picture of a pineapple. Then I would suggest that you procure from a dye company a formula of the correct dyes to use in combination, and you could experiment with your own dye pot.

Unless you have had experience in painting a pineapple with oils, a realistic colored picture is your best guide.

Begin your hooking at section 1, hooking the little scalelike center first. Then hook shadow as indicated on drawing, first around the right side, then around the left side. Follow directional hooking lines from edge toward center. Do not outline the edge, for that would destroy the contour.

Finish each section as you progress, watching your shadows and highlights. In hooking the green leaves at top of pineapple, notice that 2 is a rollover; hook this first, as shown in chapter on leaves. For remaining leaves follow directional hooking lines, noting shadows and highlights.

Fig. 81.

❦ 18 ❧

Instruction for Hooking Vegetables

FIG. 82.

LETTUCE

Hook stem end of lettuce first, with White and Light Yellowish Green.
Next, hook leaf 1 in same Yellowish Green shades, following directional

hooking lines shown in Fig. 82. Please follow the directions for hooking leaves as given in Chapter 12. With all the instruction you have received up to this point, you should have no difficulty.

GREEN PEAS

Start at 1, Fig. 83, hooking the pea as though it were the top of a grape (Chapter 17). Watch your curved hooking to make roundness. Hook peas to the right and then to the left of 1, watching the contour. Use the same shades in all the peas. Then hook area 2 in the inside of the pod. Note the shadow behind the peas and on the edge of the pod. Follow directional hooking lines. In area 3, the outside of the pod, hook as the lines direct. *Do not outline.*

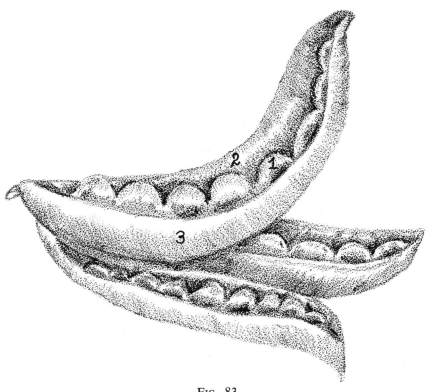

FIG. 83.

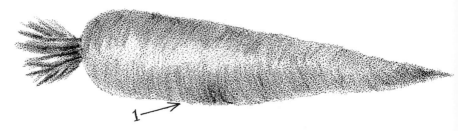

FIG. 84.

CARROT

As suggested under the banana, I recommend following a picture of a carrot for correct colors. Start hooking at 1, edge of carrot, making short, curved shadow lines along the lower edge of the carrot as illustrated. Repeat on upper side and fill in between with palest shade of Carrot color.

Instruction for Hooking Chain and Ribbon Bow

CHAIN

In making a chain, reason that a part of each link is in back of the one on each side. Note shadows at A and also a lesser shadow at B in each link. Follow directional hooking lines. Place highlight in center length of each link.

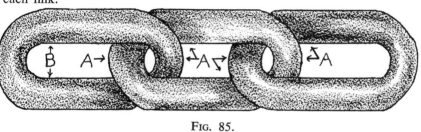

FIG. 85.

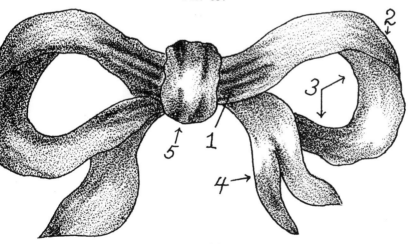

FIG. 86.

RIBBON BOW

In hooking a ribbon bow, start at 1 where the bow comes out of the

163

center tie. Notice the shading and wrinkles and distance of shadow. Next, hook your lightest shade through the center of the bow, to the right as far as 2, just as you did through the center of each link in the chain. Repeat on top of left-hand bow. Then, hook lower loop of right-hand bow at 3, noting the shadows which occur because this is the inside of the loop. Hook end of ribbon 4, noting placement of shadows. Repeat on lower half of left-hand bow. Last, hook the "tie" 5 as shown, with shadows and wrinkles. Always follow Stratton method of directional lines with no outline.

Fig. 87.   Design No. 295, "Cocker Spaniel," hooked by Mrs. Marie Kerslake, Turners Falls, Massachusetts

Fig. 88. Frost Design No. 72, hooked by Mrs. Ruth Nickerson, Har-
wich, Massachusetts

✥ 20 ✥

Instruction for Hooking Turkish Orientals

Since Oriental rugs were first imported into this country they have been admired and desired by millions of people.

Being laboriously hand woven, the genuine antique Orientals have been so expensive as to be beyond the reach of many families. Hookers have overcome this difficulty by making their own.

Now, what is it about Orientals that so attracts the eye and pleases the senses? Probably not the motifs which, though they all have a reference to the religion or family life of the country in which they are made, are not especially attractive.

Disregarding the design you have only the colors left and the subtle combination of color is the attraction. They do not conflict with other room decorations but blend with them and each enhances the beauty of the other.

In your floral and scroll hooked rugs your color schemes are almost unlimited, and the depth or brilliancy of the colors is much more pronounced than in Orientals, where all colors are muted. In my opinion, if you plan to hook an Oriental pattern the result will be much more pleasing to you if you follow the color plan of the particular country from which your design originated rather than using colors which you personally like.

I suggest that you go to your local library and study the authoritative books on Orientals which you will find there. Color plates appear in most of them and these will give you ideas of the correct colors to use in the particular design you have chosen. You will learn that the weaver's whole family worked on the rugs and the errors in the weaving were caused by temperament or emotional disturbances of the weaver. In true Orientals these variations in design do not lessen the value but may in some cases increase it.

CHARACTERISTICS OF TURKISH RUGS

The distinguishing characteristics of old Turkish rugs are the bright color effects, in general brighter than the Persian rugs, and the use of much Canary, Lavender, Mauve, with the Reds and light Blues. The Reds are not the Blue Reds but rather the Brownish Reds that have Yellow in them. Also Olive Greens, dark to pale, Off White, Tan and Aqua Blue were used. These rugs use rectangular lines and a great massing of colors. Animal and human motifs were never used because it was against their religion. Perhaps half of these old rugs were in prayer designs. Each type has a prayer niche, which is the part of the design showing the *mihrab* or niche in the wall of the mosque and so located on the rug that when the worshiper prostrates himself before it he will be facing toward Mecca.

It is interesting to note that the first Oriental hooked rug patterns were introduced by Mr. E. S. Frost of Biddeford, Maine. He manufactured the first hooked rug patterns to be sold commercially in this country and advertised the Orientals in his little descriptive catalogue as "Copies of the latest importations of Turkish Rugs." It would seem, therefore, that rugs from Persia, India, and other countries were not being imported at that time as all the Frost Orientals are definitely Turkish in origin.

Turkish rugs are divided into three separate and entirely different groups. Group 1 is composed of antique and semi-antique rugs made prior to World War I. Group 2 comprises the hundreds of thousands of cheap copies of the old types that were made after World War I and up to about 1932. Group 3 are rugs made in Turkey after World War I in carpet sizes that copied or attempted to copy the Persian designs. Most of the motifs in Turkish rugs are geometric in form.

FROST TURKISH ORIENTAL DESIGN NO. 116

FIG. 89. Frost design No. 116

As a concrete example of an authentic Turkish design I am giving you Frost Design No. 116 with suggested colors gleaned from my many years' study of Orientals.

Outside straight border: Hook single row of Black on the outside line of border. Hook single row of Navy Blue on inside line of border. This helps keep the whole border in position; then fill in with straight rows of Navy Blue. At each corner of any right-angle design do not hook around the corner but end each of the lines at a diagonal or miter line to give a sharp-cornered effect.

As the pattern is mounted on your frame you are facing one end of the design; therefore, instruction from here on will be from the end toward the center.

Note: There is no definite formula for colors to be used in the very small motifs of Turkish Orientals, but watch out and repeat the choice of colors or tints occasionally all through the design. Please notice that the general design on Turkish Orientals, with the exception of prayer rugs, repeats at the center so that you only have to plan one half of the design.

Hook the two seven-point motifs attached to outside border as follows: Hook the stem and small center in muted Oliver Green using about the 3rd shade. In the remainder of the figures use Aqua Blue of 4th shade from light. To separate the petals, outline with Navy Blue.

All Orientals have much contrast outlining around motifs which blend into background.

For the seven-pointed motif with center facing the hooker, same shape as Fig. 90, I suggest you outline with Maroon and fill in with beautiful Rose Red, Oriental Shade. Background for this area could be a medium shade of Old Blue, 3rd or 4th shade.

Background for this border area could be a Brick Maroon. (*Caution:* do not use a Rose Red.) Hook in your usual method but in straight lines.

Next you have an irregular double banded secondary border. For first line, hook one single line of 3rd light shade of Seal Brown. Outline the middle line of this band with Navy Blue. Fill in between with Paisley or a fine mixture giving the same effect.

Outline inside edge of band with Navy Blue, filling in with a medium shade of Deep Bright Red.

For border of small rectangular panel, outline with Navy Blue, edging on outside with one line of faded Aqua Blue. This with the Navy Blue will run all around the center panel. Fill in with 3rd shade of dull Aqua Blue.

For center figure in small rectangle, outline with off-White of light shade of Seal Brown. Fill in with Paisley, a Mixture or fine Plaid that has coloring of Maroons and Reds.

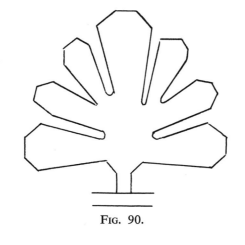

Fig. 90.

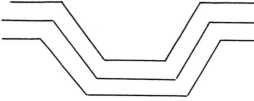

Fig. 91.

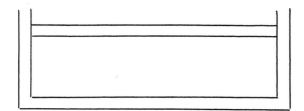

Fig. 92.

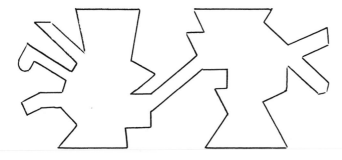

Fig. 93.

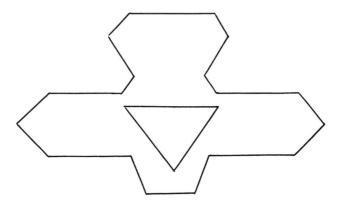

Fig. 94.

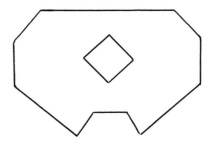

Fig. 95.

For motifs on each side of center motif, outline triangle in center with Olive Green. Inside of this, one line of Old Gold, filling in with 3rd shade of Grey Blue. Outline the figure in which the triangle lies with Navy Blue. Fill in with 3rd or 4th shade of Aqua Blue. Background of this panel: medium shade of Taupe Sand.

For motif on which little square lies, outline with Navy Blue with one row of light Soft Blue inside the Navy. Fill in to the inside square with Paisley or Brick Red mixture. Outline the little square with Navy Blue and one row of Old Gold, making two outlines. Fill in with medium Aqua Blue.

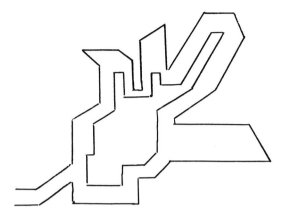

Fig. 96.

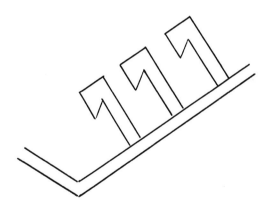

Fig. 97.

The next motif is in center of triangular shaped corners. For center motif, outline with Off White, fill in with 3rd shade of Red Grape. For outside line, outline with Gold and fill with medium shade of Olive Green.

For straight lines to which hook designs are attached, outline with Navy Blue. Next to upper line, one row of good rich Red. Fill in with medium shade Dark Sand. Outline hooks with Maroon, fill in with Paisley.

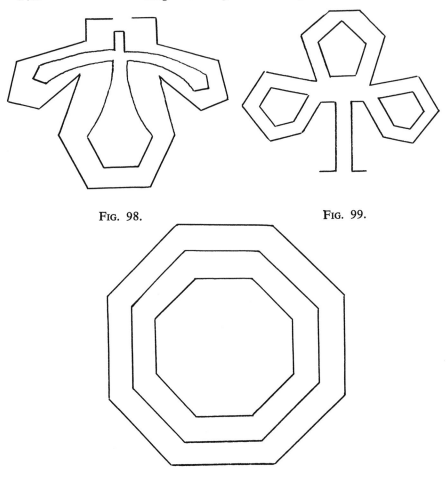

Fig. 98.   Fig. 99.

Fig. 100.

Lower part of large center design. Outline with 2nd shade Aqua Blue. Outline inside figure with light shade Olive Green, fill in with Paisley or soft Mixture already used. Repeat these colors in the figures on each side of one just hooked and on other end of center.

For upper section of the center motif, outline three small centers with Navy Blue. Fill in with Mixture previously used. Outside three motifs, outline with 1st light shade Aqua Blue. Fill in with original Aqua Blue shade used in first border. This is repeated in other motifs of same shape.

For center octagon, outline with Old Gold, filling in with soft Olive Green or your Mixture or with Paisley. Outline the outside octagon with Navy Blue. Fill in with Rose Red. Background, Light Beige. Be sure it harmonizes with other Tans previously used.

FIG. 101.

ONE HALF OF FROST TURKISH PATTERN NO. 108

This design is one of the best of the Frost Orientals and is available in two sizes; the larger one is 40½ x 76½ inches; on the smaller one the very outside border is omitted. Also, surrounded by eight repeats of Fig. 113, it comes in an even larger size, 76 x 112 inches.

The illustrated motifs and suggested colors given for each begin on the end of the design and work toward the center.

For outside border, hook one row Black on both outside and inside lines. Fill in with rows of Navy Blue, mitering the corners.

FIG. 102.

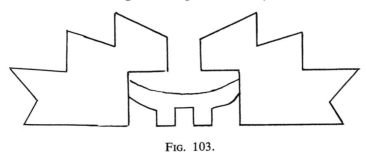

FIG. 103.

Pointed motifs in first outside band. Outline two center double figures (Fig. 103 done twice) with Navy Blue, making four pointed figures. Fill in with straight rows of about the 3rd shade of Aqua Blue. Figure connecting each double unit; outline with Black, fill with medium shade Olive Green. For the two double figures on the right of the center pair, outline with Navy Blue, fill with a beautiful, soft Oriental Red of about 3rd dark shade. Repeat on left of center. Connecting figures, same as above. This follows all around the rug. Background, dark Brownish Maroon. *Caution*— Turkish Maroon has a Brown not Blue tint.

Four-line inner border: Outline first row Black, following with Royal Blue, Black on next line, one line each of Red and Orchid; next, Black, Olive Green, Old Gold and Black on last line. Directly beyond the last Black, I used one line of Off White. These colors follow all around the rug.

Pointed motifs in first outside band: Outline two center double figures Fig. 103, but with Red above the Aqua and Aqua above the Red of the first border. Connecting figure same as lower border figure, Olive Green. Background medium shade Grey Blue.

FIG. 104.

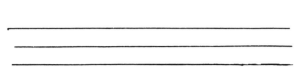

Fig. 105.

Hook the three lines similarly to lower four lines but directly below first line hook one row of Off White.

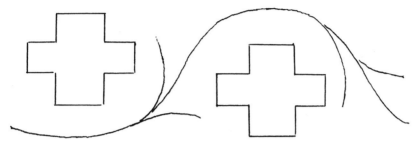

Fig. 106.

Small crosses in third border: Outline each cross with Navy Blue. Fill in with Paisley, alternating each line of Paisley with two or three shades of Blue, Old Gold, Red and Olive Green. Hook wavy lines of the vine with Olive Green. Background, 3rd shade light Seal Brown or light Sand.

Fig. 107.

Double line on lower side of fourth border: Outline with Navy Blue and fill in with Paisley or any of the colors used below in the banding strips. Follow this all around the panel.

Fig. 108.

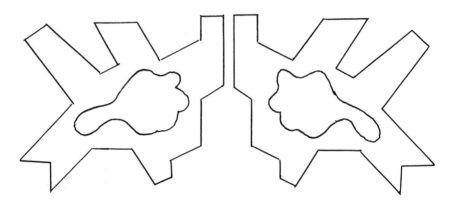

Fig. 109.

Small squarish motifs: Outline with Maroon, fill in with Plum, Red, Light and Medium Blues, Aquas, Turquoise or Orchids, placing the colors as you choose, all around the panel. For three short lines between small irregular squares: upper and lower lines, Deep Red; center line Aqua. Background, tint of palest Grey Blue. Double line on upper side, same as lower line.

For motifs inside of panel: Center double figure, outline with Navy Blue, fill in with Pale Light Blue. Outline small center figure with Navy Blue, fill in with Paisley.

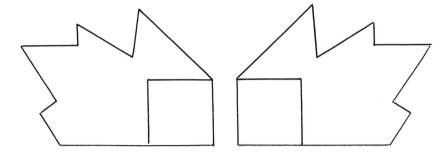

FIG. 110.

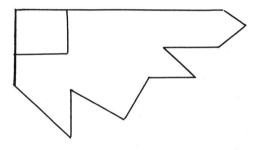

FIG. 111.

Two motifs above center: Outline with Navy Blue, fill in with Aqua used in first and second borders. Small square at corner of these figures: fill in with Paisley or Mixture.

Next motif to left on lower part of panel: Outline with Navy Blue, fill in with Green Plaid. Fill in square corner with Paisley.

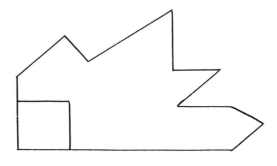

Fig. 112.

Motif directly above: Outline with Maroon, fill in with Medium Red used in first and second borders. Fill in square with Paisley.

Motif in lower left corner: Outline with Navy Blue, fill in with Light Blue.

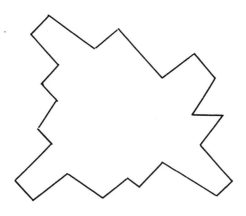

Fig. 113.

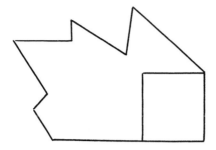

Fig. 114.

Motif above the one just made: Outline with Navy Blue, fill in with 3rd dark shade of Red Grape, with Paisley in the square corner. Background, medium shade of Grey Blue a little lighter than used in background of second border. Repeat all on right side of panel.

Motifs in left corner of center large panel: Corner design, outline with Navy Blue, fill in with Light Blue. Three small figures inside the design, outline with Navy Blue, fill in with medium Red.

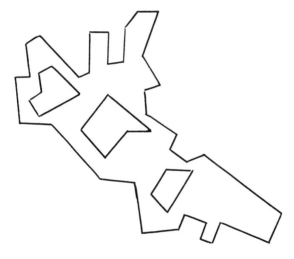

Fig. 115.

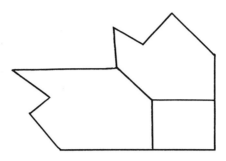

FIG. 116.

Motif on right next to corner: Outline with Navy Blue, fill in with Aqua Blue as used previously. Small square with Paisley or Mixture. For other two similar motifs above: Outline all with Navy Blue, fill the square with Paisley or Mixture, and the rest of figure, medium Red.

Outline with Navy Blue, fill with medium Aqua Blue. Repeat five designs just described on right-hand side of pattern. Background for this corner section, rich Dark Plum.

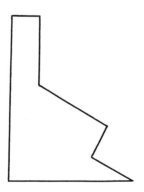

FIG. 117.

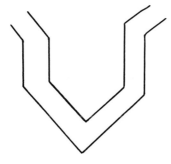

FIG. 118.

Irregular border: One row each of Navy Blue, Aqua, Red and Navy Blue.

"Running Hooks": Outline with Navy Blue, fill in with Paisley or medium Red mixture. Background, Light Beige used on *third border*.

Five motifs: Outline all with Off White or pale tint of Pink. Middle figure, fill in with medium Red. Small leaf in center, use Green Plaid as used below. Two figures at each side of the center one; fill in with Aqua. For the two remaining figures; fill with medium Red.

FIG. 119.

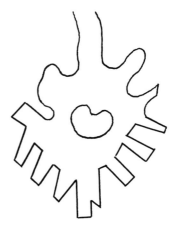

FIG. 120.

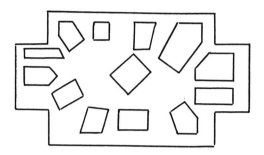

Fig. 121.

Notched corner medallions (ten in all): Outline with Navy Blue. Use same colors as in border number four. Background for each, Blue of second border. The three bands connecting the medallions, use Navy Blue on all four lines. In between, Red, Aqua, Gold, Olive Green, Medium Blue.

Small motifs joining center medallion to large cross: Outline with Navy Blue, fill in with medium Red.

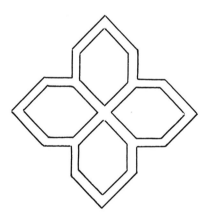

Fig. 122.

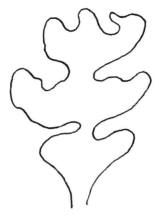

Fig. 123.

Large four-point geometric center: Outline outside edge and second line in with Navy Blue, fill space between with Paisley. Four inside plaques: Outline with Navy Blue, fill in with Aqua Blue used in borders.

Surrounding band: Use same Blue shade as in end panel above the fourth border.

❧ 21 ❧

Instruction for Hooking Persian Orientals

Persian rugs differ from Turkish in that they use the floral designs and large medallions more frequently. Often both floral and medallion motifs are highly conventionalized and are, in effect, geometric, although the floral influence is always present. Many of the Persian weavers still follow the traditional designs used by their ancestors hundreds of years ago. One of the most interesting points about designs is the manner in which the Persian weavers obtain certain color effects. A study of these rugs will show you that each design is bounded by a color, sometimes so fine as to be almost invisible. Yet it has an extraordinary effect on the color it encloses.

Persian rugs are identified by being given the name of the city or section of the country in which they were made, such as Hamadan, Kirman, Kurdistan or Sarouk. More than half of all available Persian scatter rugs come from in and around Hamadan. As these rugs are made in scores of villages as well as in the city of Hamadan, there are many variations in design. The Persian rugs as a class have deteriorated less in quality than rugs from Turkey and other countries.

Ninety per cent of all Oriental rugs sold in America and Europe come from Persia, now known as Iran. They are outstanding in the combination of colors, beauty of design, and workmanship. The "knot" used by the Persians is finer than the Turkish "knot" thereby producing a somewhat smoother surface.

Persian designs include curved scroll-type figures and floral motifs with once in a while birds or animals. Colors are varied, but soft and more subdued than the Turkish colors.

To assist the maker of a "hand hooked" Oriental, I am giving the details of coloring in my Persian Oriental Design No. 440 which has become so popular with hookers.

Fig. 124. Detail of Design No. 440, showing one quarter of center medallion. The colors recommended are keyed to the numbers in the drawing, as follows: 1—Maroon. 2—Light Beige. 3—Off-White. 4—Navy Blue. 5—Old Gold. 6—Olive Green. 7—Rose Red. 8—Paisley. 9—Old Blue. 10—Light Blue. 11—Light Pink. 12—Medium Blue.

FIG. 125.

FIG. 126.

FIG. 127.

Since the pattern is mounted on your frame with the end toward you, directions for colors begin at the end and work toward the center of the design.

FIG. 128.

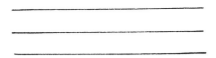

FIG. 129.

FIG. 130.

Border band: Outer line, outline with Navy Blue, inner line Old Gold. Fill between with Navy Blue. This method produces a more even border band.

Fig. 131.

Fig. 132.

FIG. 133.

FIG. 134.

FIG. 135.

FIG. 136.

FIGURED BORDER

Left-hand corner motif: Outline with Off White, fill in six petals with medium shade Light Blue, fill in small center with Gold and Olive Green. Repeat in other three corners.

Conventionalized leaf: Paisley vein, balance of leaf area, Olive Green. Repeat in other three corners.

There are fourteen of these motifs in this border.

Hook all scrolls with Olive Green. Start at left-hand corner: Outline six-petal flower with Navy Blue, fill petals with 3rd light shade of Red Grape, fill small center with Gold and Olive Green. Same figure at right of one just hooked: Outline six-petal flower with Navy Blue, fill petals with Old Gold, fill center with Red mixture. Alternate these colors around the rug in this figured border.

Background for figured border: 3rd dark shade of Rose Red.

There are twelve sets of the motifs in this border. Outline each of them with Olive Green and fill with Gold.

Lower and middle lines Navy Blue. Fill with Old Gold and Rose Red. Inside line, Pastel Green, fill with Gold and Medium Blue.

Palm in corner: Outline with Navy Blue, fill in with either Paisley or Red mixture or medium Olive Green. Six-petal motif inside: Outline with Maroon, fill in with medium shade Rose Red, center Olive Green. Two buds attached to palm; Olive Green base, Rose Red top.

Five-petal small unit: Outline with Navy Blue, fill with Old Gold. Fill center with medium Blue. Leaf design: leaves and base of bud, Olive Green, tip of bud Rose Red.

Ribbon crossing corner: Inside line Off White, outside line Navy Blue. Fill with Paisley or similar Mixture.

Background for whole corner section, Light Beige.

Motif on side: Outline with Navy Blue, fill in with Olive Green.

Outline with Old Gold, fill with Olive Green.

Flower at center of each end: Outline Oval with Navy Blue. Outline seven-petal flower with medium Light Blue, with Paisley center. Background Light Beige.

22

Story of the Yankee Peddler, Edward Sands Frost

Hooked rugs started from a humble beginning but now grace the floors of beautiful homes furnished with valuable pieces of antique furniture. It has been suggested that, like Cinderella, they rose from a place by the hearth to unexpected glory.

It was not until about 1867 that rug hookers were relieved of one step in the making of their rugs, namely, the drafting of the design. To many it may have been a relief only because it allowed that much more time for the other details. Some continued to draw their own designs, and many do so even to this day.

This relief from design drawing was made possible by an ingenious Yankee named Frost who manufactured the first known commercial hooked rug pattern. His efforts to produce something that the housewives could purchase at a very moderate price and the results of those efforts make a story in themselves. Because he was a pioneer in this phase of the art, and because the designs he sold have stood the test of the years, a brief history of his life is worth repeating. It has been recorded by various writers.

Edward Sands Frost was born in Biddeford, Maine, January 1, 1843. He attended the schools of Biddeford, where he was known as a keen-minded boy with a leaning toward things mechanical. This leaning influenced him as a young man to study the trade of machinist. He became an expert and in later years this skill was of very material assistance in making his rug patterns.

At the outbreak of the Civil War he enlisted in Company E of the First Maine Cavalry for active service. At the close of the war he returned to Biddeford, where he resumed work as a machinist. When ill health forced him to give up this work, on the advice of his physician, he took up the business of a tin peddler in order to be out of doors more than was possible as a machinist. He plied this trade through Maine, parts of New Hampshire and Massachusetts, going from village to village and farm to farm with a supply of everything our grandmothers needed, from calico to tinware.

191

FIG. 137. Frost Design No. 68, hooked by Mrs. Ora Kimberley, Springfield, Massachusetts

Fɪɢ. 138.　Frost Design No. 6, hooked by Mrs. Beth Cutler, Barre, Vermont

Mr. Frost became a personal friend of his customers, since he had time to stop and rest a bit and carry news from one house to another. He bargained with his customers for old rags and old copper wash boilers, little realizing at the time that the copper bottoms of the wash boilers would be particularly useful to him later.

He evidently was of an artistic nature. During his visits with his customers, where he often stayed overnight, he noticed many housewives hooking rugs on material on which they or their neighbors had drawn their own designs. Being a shrewd Yankee trader and always looking for more business, he conceived the idea of making patterns himself to sell to his trade. Living in a fair-sized town he would be able to procure a burlap of better quality than the teasacking then being used. So he gave calico or tinware for the rugs he desired to copy and upon his return to Biddeford he would study how to make a permanent pattern from which to stamp burlaps to be sold to his customers. He finally decided that metal was the only lasting material to use.

His first pattern was in outline only, using two plates to produce a continuous line. It is recorded that the first pattern so cut took thirty days to produce, as it was all hand work with cold chisel and hammer. One of these first patterns is in the group I now own.

It was not until later that he developed the method of stamping in color by the use of multiple plates. Here was where the old copper bottoms from his collection of wash boilers came into their own, for a time at least. But, using small pieces of copper with but one or two figures cut in each piece, it was difficult to stamp two patterns just alike. The remedy for this problem was to cut the whole design from sheets of metal the size of the finished pattern. Copper in large sheets not being obtainable at a reasonable figure, he turned to zinc as a proper substitute.

He cut the full size of the figures from one plate, shading marks from another, leaves from one or two more, veins and accent marks from others until some patterns would require six or eight plates to produce the finished article. This type of pattern seemed to please the ladies and business boomed. Burlaps sold at thirty cents, fifty cents, eighty cents, but none over a dollar. Remember, this was in the 1870's when a dollar was worth one hundred cents.

The development of a design, the decision as to what to cut out from each plate and the actual cutting must have been a colossal undertaking.

Not all of Mr. Frost's patterns were pleasing, but as a group they were, in 1878, awarded first prize "For the best and handsomest patterns manufactured," by Mechanics Fair in Boston and by American Institute Fair in New York.

However, Mr. Frost himself did not receive this honor in person as the business had been sold to the Mayor of Biddeford, Mr. James H. Strout,

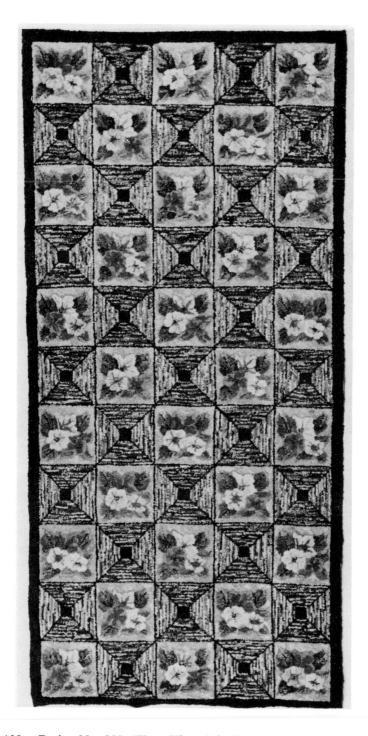

FIG. 139. Design No. 308, "Kent Hit-or-Miss," hooked by Mrs. Stella Sell-
berg, Barre, Vermont

two years before. Mr. Frost, again in poor health, had been taken to California on a stretcher. The Western climate benefited him and he became a successful photographer.

Because of the uniqueness of the idea of rug pattern stencils and because many of the designs were outstanding, the Frost patterns have been of interest to hookers and to writers on hooking for many years.

There has been some speculation as to the origin of the designs used by Mr. Frost, some crediting them to his own artistic ability and some to the housewives upon whom he called in plying his trade as a peddler. Probably both statements are true in part but interesting facts on the subject have come into my possession which were heretofore not generally known.

During the operation of my Montpelier, Vermont, Studio a group of ladies from Haverhill, Massachusetts, arrived while a class was in full swing and they seemed very interested in everything they saw.

One lady introduced herself as Mrs. Florence K. Peel, and she said her interest in coming to my studio was to see the Frost stencils in which she felt a rather personal interest. As the story was told me by Mrs. Peel, her grandmother, Mrs. Robert Benson, was one of Biddeford's leading ladies. Her husband was a skilled man who was overseer in the York mills in Saco and Biddeford and an expert on dyeing.

The Bensons were well-to-do people and their home was an old mansion which sat high on a hill overlooking the Saco River. The house was full of many fine pieces of old furniture, blown glass and carved marble as well as much fine linen. Grandma Benson possessed much creative ability, and she loved color. Her beautiful flower garden was resplendent with cabbage roses, poppies, calla lilies, fuchsias, and borders of ladies' delight.

Her artistic nature found expression in planning her own designs for the rugs she hooked. First she would determine the desired size of a rug and draw this border on a large sheet of paper. Selecting a large cabbage rose from her garden, she would lay it on the paper and draw around it to get the exact size and shape. She followed the same plan with the other flowers and leaves, placing them where her artistic eye told her they should be. She often used berries and acorns in her designs and frequently made geometric patterns in full design. To fill the unused corner areas she copied the scrolls from her old clocks and furniture.

Having completed the drawing it was ready to be transferred to the home-spun linen that was used as the foundation, or for making a duplicate.

Grandpa Benson was interested in these rugs too and, laying the pattern on the floor, he would study it with Grandma. Together they would plan the colors, all true to nature, and from the mills he would bring the damaged or torn pieces of pure wool cloth for Grandma to use.

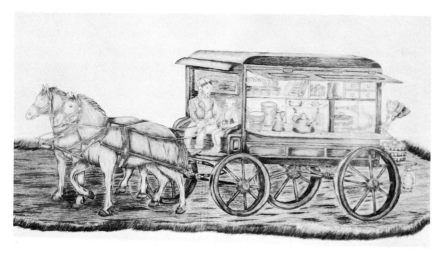

FIG. 140. "My Recollection of a Yankee Peddler," drawing by the author

Her technique of hooking varied. Some strips were cut very fine, and the loops were not clipped. Others, particularly the flower designs, were hooked with a wider strip and each loop cut, thus letting the colors melt into each other, giving the finished rug a really velvety appearance.

In those days, "tin peddler day" was something everyone looked forward to, and Grandma Benson was no exception. Being a very hospitable woman she offered everyone who came into her home a cup of tea and pie, cake or cookies. Mr. Frost was probably so entertained and he made many a prolonged business call, chatting about his wares and about the usual neighborhood gossip.

Mr. Frost had always shown an interest in Grandma Benson's hooked rugs, as they seemed to him the most beautiful he had ever seen.

On one of his visits he made Grandma Benson an offer for all of her hooked rugs. Mrs. Peel, my informant, did not know what the offer was but it was sufficiently attractive to cause Grandma Benson to accept it. All of her rugs were loaded into Mr. Frost's peddler cart and taken to Biddeford. There Mr. Frost copied the designs onto his sheets of zinc and laboriously cut the designs with cold chisel and hammer.

I am deeply grateful to Mrs. Peel for these facts and it gives me great pleasure to record them permanently in this book.

In my opinion this information, as given me by Mrs. Peel, definitely establishes the fact that, although this group of old patterns are spoken of as Frost designs, they were not conceived by Mr. Frost but were copies of designs originally drawn by the housewives. None of Mr. Frost's old catalogues makes any claim that he originated the designs, and in fact the Oriental designs were frankly acknowledged to be "copies of the latest importations of Turkish Rugs," which the ship captains had brought from the old countries.

23

My Studios in Montpelier and Greenfield and Other Activities

Prior to the acquisition of the Frost stencils my studio in Montpelier, Vermont, was known as the Old New England Hooked Rug Studio. The patterns I then sold were those of my own design or copies of fine old rugs.

The Frost designs, being a definite group by themselves, required a special identification. So my studio was renamed and has since been known as The Yankee Peddler Hooked Rug Studio in addition to the Old New England title.

And, from this title, my "Yankee Peddler Pageant" received its name. It is appropriate, indeed, as the pageant includes many rugs of the Frost designs.

In my Vermont studio, classes were held six days of each week and, because of the earnest desire of the pupils to learn the best selections of colors and the finest shading possible, the rugs produced in that studio are among the most beautiful hooked rugs in the country.

From my experience and training in art, I contributed much through my instruction. But the real success of the finished work was due to the ability of the hookers to apply to their hooking the knowledge they had acquired and to produce with their hands, not mine, the rugs of which we were all so justly proud.

The studio always welcomed visitors, many of whom came from distant states. Pupils were so pleased with the atmosphere of the studio, that they continued to come to class for sixteen years. Vacancies were caused only by death or changes of residence to some distant point.

The chairmen of my first four classes were Mrs. Abbie L. Starkey and Mrs. Mabel Hunt of Montpelier, Vermont, and Mrs. Arthur Sprague and the late Mrs. George Kent of Barre, Vermont. These four were still acting as my chairmen when my studio was closed, and Mrs. Starkey has been teaching excellent rug work since then.

I wish it were possible to reproduce photos of the hundreds of hookers who attended classes at my studio, but space will not permit. Included here

FIG. 141. Montpelier (Vermont) class; Mrs. Abbie L. Starkey, Chairman

FIG. 142. Barre (Vermont) class: the late Mrs. George Kent, Chairman. The round, partially-completed scenic design in upper center was hooked by the lady on the left, Mrs. Robert Tracy; it is probably the finest scenic rug ever hooked.

are one class from Montpelier, and one from Barre, as representative of the whole group. The loyal support of all of my pupils has been of great assistance to me in my activities in the hooked rug field.

Upon moving to Greenfield, Massachusetts, I closed my Vermont studio and took a much needed three-year vacation. In 1950 I reopened my studio in Greenfield, where I was again fortunate in having the support and encouragement of my family and friends. My husband had retired after forty-one years of service with the National Life Insurance Co. of Vermont. Being the kind of person who could not sit down with nothing to do but twiddle his thumbs, he has acted as my treasurer and secretary. He also superintended my manufacturing when I was away on lecture tours or exhibiting my Yankee Peddler Pageant. My Vermont and Massachusetts friends have been most kind and generous in loaning their rugs for my exhibits.

A normal school for training hooked rug teachers, or hobbyists wishing to perfect their technique, has been established at the studio and has been most successful. A course of teacher training by correspondence, for those who cannot come to the studio, has become popular beyond all expectations.

A table-model folding rug frame has been developed and is filling the needs of many persons who hook only small articles or who live in such small quarters that a floor-model frame is not suitable.

My *Hooking Digest Magazine* has received excellent support, and services in pamphlet form for hookers in rural areas have proved most successful.

The cordial atmosphere of the Vermont studio still prevails at Greenfield, where all are most welcome.

24

Hooking for Brides and Planning the Type of Hooked Rugs Appropriate for Your Home

---

To every hooking mother blessed with a daughter there comes the time when she wants to hook a special bride's rug.

Mother will select a design that will lend itself nicely to the important event for which it is to be used and plan her colors with equal care. If the background can be made of Grandmother's old soft homespun blanket it will add to the sentimental value of this prized possession.

Three excellent examples of bride's rugs are shown in Color Plate III: "Antoinette's Bridal Rug"; Color Plate VIII: "Summer Bloom"; and Fig. 143: "Glenmore." I have many other equally nice ones, but lack of space prevents their reproduction here.

Now that we have taken care of the bride let us give some thought to other types of hooked rugs appropriate for her home or our own.

In planning the type of hooked rug appropriate for the various rooms of the home, consideration should be given to the colors in wallpaper, drapes, floor coverings and other accessories so that the colors used in the rug will harmonize rather than clash with them.

Personal taste is always evident, and it should be, in planning the decorations of our homes. If the home is Early American, the inside decorations other than hooked rugs may have come to you from previous generations or you may have selected them yourself. Your choice of hooked rug designs to brighten and add colors and warmth will be as carefully chosen.

Your living room will propably receive your greater attention, but, in any room, use your rugs for the same purpose as you do the pictures and flower bouquets: color properly placed. If you have a fireplace, an oval or rectangular rug is suitable, though many prefer a half-round such as my Vermont Fireplace Rug shown in Color Plate No. II.

Before the sofa or davenport a less showy design will soften the general effect and complement the other decorations. With a neutral-shade broadloom as a background your rugs will be displayed to great advantage. Or, the wide pine-board floor of a very old house serves as a very beautiful resting place for the old designs. Many of these designs were preserved for posterity by Edward Sands Frost, as described in Chapter 22.

For bedrooms, floral, geometric or conventional designs are always suitable. Jimmy's or Mary's room might boast a nursery, a puppy or a kitty design hooked with some of the colors now in the draperies.

The cold tile or wood floor of the bathroom may be warmed and brightened with a hooked rug depicting a scene of the seashore with a light-blue sky and green tinted water and perhaps a white swan or sea gull in the center.

We must not forget the entrance hall and stairway. If you like a welcome mat at the door, as many do, you should choose a design that is

FIG. 143. Design No. 375, "Glenmore," hooked by Mrs. Mildred B. Kohr, Cheverly, Maryland

quiet and subdued in its color scheme. A pretty scroll design, if carefully planned and executed, will attract attention but will not detract from other hall decorations if muted colors from the wallpaper are used. A very pretty rug of this type is shown in Fig. 59, "Doorway Favorite."

If you do not care for the welcome mat type of rug, a leaf design will furnish a most pleasing effect if a neutral, semi-light background is used.

For the stair carpet there is rather a wide range of designs. In this case, personal taste is generally more definite than in the choice of designs for other places in the house. There are, of course, fewer hookers with the courage to tackle seven or eight yards of hooking. This situation has been altered somewhat by the fact that I have stair carpet designs printed with one tread and one riser on a burlap. This eliminates the heavy roll of burlap on your frame and when all sets are completed they may be sewed together in one long strip or tacked on tread and base of risers. Examples of these are shown in Figs. 69 and 70. A pleasing continuous design is my pattern "Mountain Maple," shown in Fig. 144.

FIG. 144.   Mountain-maple design

FIG. 145.   Design No. 288

Fig. 146. Mixed Borders Design

If your home is of modern structural design, undoubtedly your furnishings are also modern but colors in drapes, upholstery, wallpaper, etc., will not be much different from those in older houses.

For the living room or dining room, geometric, conventional or even contemporary designs are desired rather than the floral type. A geometric design such as my design No. 288, the principal motif of which is shown

Fig. 147. Artists' squares design

in Fig. 145, is most pleasing. If you care for the contemporary type of design, the mixed borders (Fig. 146) and Artists' Squares (Fig. 147) could be very attractive.

I trust my suggestions on planning hooked rugs for your home will be helpful to you and I wish you all success.

25

Contentment and Friendship in Hooking

I have such strong feelings about the contentment derived from hooking and the friendships made through the associations with other hookers I could not resist the temptation to include the picture here shown, which was sent me by one of my good customers, as an example of what is taking place all over this country of ours. The pleasure, pride in their work and contentment in their efforts are so graphically expressed on each face.

To this group of ladies, like thousands of other similar groups, their hooking is a hobby in which they become so intensely interested they hardly know when it is time to go to bed. And in lots of cases Mother's enthusiam is unconsciously transferred to other members of the family.

Soon Mother is hooking the design and the children and even Dad are helping out with the background. This participation increases their interest in rug hooking to a point where they each have a pattern of their own and they hook the whole thing, sometimes even better than Mother does.

When rug hooking was new in this country the hobby idea hadn't been thought of. The usefulness of the finished rug was the compelling force. As "time was of the essence," the rugs were generally made as quickly as possible and in such colors and types of material as were at hand. Regardless of this general situation there were some mothers with more time at their disposal, and with a more artistic nature than others, who took more pains in shading their flowers and scrolls.

Today the necessity angle of rug hooking is of minor importance, and the hobby idea is paramount. The time element being eliminated, much more attention can be given subtle and careful execution of the design. Artistic temperaments can be indulged to a much more extensive degree. Careful graduated shading of all parts of the design produces an artistic whole that is very pleasing to its creator.

I have observed the indulgence in hobbies of many different kinds but few of them have ever enjoyed the wide-spread acceptance that has been given to rug hooking. And it seems to lend itself to the occupational therapy angle so nicely. Patients in veterans' hospitals are encouraged to make

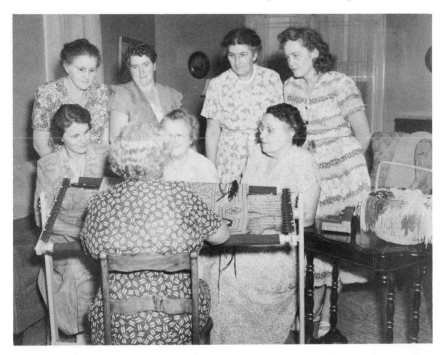

FIG. 148. Group of rug hookers at Northboro, Massachusetts, Mrs. Sophie Lawrence (lady with back to camera), teacher. Seated (l. to r.): Mrs. Ruth Mayberry, Mrs. Susie Spring (over 80 years old), Mrs. John Schleyer. Standing (l. to r.): Mrs. Gordon Walker, Mrs. John Symonds, Mrs. Emma Duhamel, Mrs. Norman Schleyer.

hooked rugs, mats or small articles to assist recovery of injured muscles in hands or arms.

We all need hobbies as a relief from worries and cares that sooner or later come to most of us. I remember a remark made by the vice president of a large insurance company, whose hobby was wrought-iron work. He said, "A hobby is good for anyone even though it is no more than the study of elephants."

Perhaps best of all is that hooking is not confined to rugs alone; there are so many other articles that can be hooked: pictures for wall adornment, table mats, chair seats and hand or shopping bags. And the opportunities for self-expression in execution are almost unlimited. Designs to suit all tastes, floral, scroll or combinations of both, scenic, geometric and even Orientals all lend themselves to this hooking hobby.

The parlor, at one time used only for weddings and funerals, has now been replaced by the spacious living room. This is a gathering spot where hooking can be enjoyed by all of the family, provided the chips are cleaned up afterward.

In such a living room there surely lives contentment. May we each and all find a hobby and pursue it with every energy we possess.

Photo by Ralph Trumbull

FIG. 149.   Mr. and Mrs. Joseph Owen of Schenectady, N. Y., radiate content-ment in their mutual hobby, hooking rugs. Mr. Owen is an engineer with the General Electric Company. He finds time to work with his wife. He is hooking a galleon, while Mrs. Owen hooks my pattern of begonias. Mrs. Owen also designed and painted the picture on the wall. She intends to have it transferred to burlap and hook it. The table in the foreground has a ceramic top, designed and made by Mr. Owen.

Index